The Art of Accompaniment

Practical Steps for the Seminary Formator

Sister Marysia Weber, RSM, DO, MA

Special appendix from
Sister Joseph Marie Ruessmann, RSM, JD,
JCD, MBA

En Route Books and Media, LLC
5705 Rhodes Avenue
St. Louis, MO 63109

Cover credit: TJ Burdick

Library of Congress Control Number:
2018956342

ISBN-13: 978-1-7325949-1-3
ISBN-10: 1-7325949-1-0

DEDICATION

In loving memory of
Sister Joseph Marie Ruessmann, RSM, JD, JCD,
MBA, who wrote and worked on behalf of priestly
formation

TABLE OF CONTENTS

PRAISE FOR *THE ART OF ACCOMPANIMENT*

"As the new *Ratio Fundamentalis* from Rome invites us to deepen the integration of each seminarian through accompaniment in formation, Sr. Marysia Weber, RSM, brings to bear in this work her years of experience in helping priests and seminarians grow in affective maturity necessary for ministry. This little book offers very helpful insights and practical recommendations to assist seminary formators as they work one-on-one with seminarians in developing the necessary relationship of trust for their growth. Formators will learn from her how to create and take advantage of formative moments in seminary life so that the human and affective flourishing of the man can lead to a flourishing of his divine vocation."
– Bishop Andrew Cozzens, Auxiliary Bishop of the Archdiocese of Saint Paul and Minneapolis

"Sister Marysia Weber, RSM, DO, articulates clear, relevant ways for the priest formator to accompany seminarians in their formation to the ministerial priesthood. Proposing contemporary assessment questions, this book helps the formation advisor both evaluate and assist the seminarian in his growth in affective maturity. I recommend this compact book particularly because of its practicality, reflection of the Church's program of formation, and usefulness in identifying opportunities for interior growth for seminarians."

– Fr. Christopher Cooke, Director, Spiritual Year of Saint Charles Borromeo Seminary, Philadelphia.

"My colleague and friend, Sister Marysia Weber, RSM, has made an invaluable contribution to the work of priestly formation in her book, *The Art of Accompaniment.* Throughout the work, her skills as a psychiatrist are evident. Even more evident is her love and honor of the priestly vocation. The concept of accompaniment is key to every insight in the text. There simply is no longer a 'one size fits all' approach to priestly formation. Sister Marysia demonstrates both from science and theology varied and concrete ways in which more experienced priests can be both challenging and loving companions on a young man's journey to ordination and a life of service to the Church. Her chapter on 'Markers of Human Maturation' is especially helpful because it presents clear and evidence based ways of helping a candidate recognize individual strengths while not fearing to tackle frailties that could compromise his future life and ministry in the priesthood. The chapter on communication skills is most compelling because it helps formators know how to phrase insights in ways that are acceptable to candidates. Sister Marysia clearly grasps the truth of the old adage, 'I don't say what I say; I say what you hear.' The clearest and most objective evaluation I can give to *The Art of Accompaniment* is to say that I wish I had this book at hand when I began my own work in priestly formation decades ago. It is a significant and contemporary help in forming candidates for the priesthood after the mind of Christ, possessed of self-knowledge, and ready to serve the Church in our challenging times."

– Rev. Msgr. Thomas G. Caserta (Former Director of Spiritual Formation, Cathedral Seminary Residence within the Diocese of Brooklyn, NY, and Pastor, St. Bernadette Church, Brooklyn, NY)

Sister Marysia Weber, RSM

ACKNOWLEDGMENTS

Interactions with seminary formators, rectors and bishops over the past several decades have contributed to the contents of this book. The first chapter, *Forming Seminary Formators in the Art of Accompaniment,* offers practical means to provide, as articulated in the recent *Ratio,* the "right kind of accompaniment" required of a formator. Chapter two, *Markers of Human Maturation in Seminary Formation,* offers formators a tool to assess the presence of maturation milestones significant to priestly formation. Chapter three, *Communication Skills for Formative Dialogue Directed Toward Missionary Discipleship,* presents dialogue skills which will assist the formator in guiding the seminarian to a greater awareness "of his condition, of the talents that he has received, and of his frailties, so that he can become ever more receptive to the action of grace." (*Ratio,* no. 46). Chapter four contains templates to guide formators in their assessment of seminarians based on the principles presented. There is also a practicum exercise for formators on the art of questioning. The appendix includes the article, "Confidentiality and Knowledge Requirements in Seminary Formation" by Sister Joseph Marie Ruessmann, RSM, JD, JCD, MBA. It approaches the topic of confidentiality in seminary formation by applying the principles presented in the Church documents on priestly formation.

I am grateful to the many seminary formators for their support and encouragement in the development of this book.

FOREWORD

It would be impossible to speak of the pontificate of Pope Francis without mentioning his use of the term accompaniment. "The Church will have to initiate everyone – priests, religious, and laity – into this 'art of accompaniment' which teaches us to remove our sandals before the sacred ground of the other (cf. Ex 3:5)" (Evangelii Gaudium, 169). The art of accompaniment has become one of his overarching themes and so it follows that it is no different when he speaks of seminary formation. The seminary formator is called to accompany and journey with each man entrusted to his guidance through the seminary process. This is no mere functional role, but a genuine presence in the seminarian's life and discernment process. Sister Marysia's book offers very practical and profound ways to assist a formator as he or she begins the important work of preparing shepherds after the Heart of Christ. In fact, anyone involved in seminary formation – bishop, vocation director, faculty and even the seminarian himself – can gain a great deal of understanding through reading this book.

As the *Ratio Fundamentalis* of 2016 (The Gift of the Priestly Vocation) states: "Seminarians need to be accompanied in a personal way in the various stages of their journey by those entrusted with the work of formation, each according to his proper role and competence. The purpose of personal accompaniment is to carry out vocational discernment and to form the missionary disciple" (# 44).

Sr. Marysia helps the reader to appreciate that the seminary formation advisor's role is to be more broadly understood than just a monthly meeting. Accompaniment means knowing the man on a deep and personal level, walking alongside of him in the seminary horarium, and being with him in the joys and sorrows he experiences throughout his time in formation. As Jesus did with the disciples on the road to Emmaus, the formator recognizes that the art of accompaniment begins with an acceptance of the man where he is and a desire to see him grow and embrace the beauty and the fullness of the life to which he is being called. This process of gradualism does not happen overnight, but rather in the long and at times arduous process of formation throughout the years of seminary training.

The material comprised in this book was originally presented to a group of forty seminary formators as one of the modules within a certificate program in seminary formation that is hosted on the campus of St. Vincent de Paul Regional

Seminary in Boynton Beach, FL. Sister Marysia's presentations were exceedingly well-received and appreciated by all. Those who read these pages will walk away feeling better equipped to do the work entrusted to them. Never has there been a more important time is the church for well-balanced, affectively mature, and zealous missionary disciples preparing for the ministerial priesthood. Having been in formational work for over half of my ordained ministry, I believe this is a valuable tool that will be of great service to formators of today and tomorrow. Sister Marysia's pastoral and psychological experience render her an expert in this field, and I am grateful to her and so many in her RSM community for their contributions in the field of seminary formation.

Msgr. David L. Toups, STD
Rector/President

St. Vincent de Paul Regional Seminary
Boynton Beach, Florida

22 August 2018
The Queenship of the Blessed Virgin Mary

INTRODUCTION

The role of a seminary formator is to accompany the seminarian in the external forum and to discern with him, the seminary community, and the larger Church community whether he has a vocation to the Catholic priesthood. To accomplish this task effectively, the formator needs a vast array of skills that will enable him or her to listen to, understand, encourage, challenge, and adequately assess the seminarian in an open and honest way. This book by Sister Marysia Weber, RSM, offers many invaluable insights and practical tools that seminary formators can employ in their work.

Since a seminary formator deals primarily in the external forum, the kind of accompaniment he or she offers must differ from that typically given by a confessor or spiritual director in the internal forum. Chapter one offers five important steps the formator can take as he or she accompanies seminarians in their priestly formation: gathering background information, clarifying expectations, review of life, fostering affective growth and development, and discernment of the seminarian's suitability for the ministerial priesthood. Sister Marysia's recommendations at the end of the chapter are particularly insightful, practical, and very much to the point. She also points out how Jesus' conversation with the woman at the well (John 4:5-42) illustrates the process of accompaniment outlined in the chapter. Chapter two highlights six interrelated markers that the seminary formator should take into account when assessing the seminarian's process of human maturation: self-knowledge, self-direction, self-control, self-discipline, self-governance, and spiritual fatherhood. It describes each of these markers and includes helpful questions for assessing whether the seminarian exhibits these markers positively or only in a limited way. Chapter three identifies six important communication skills for formative dialogue that the formator can employ: reflective listening, open-ended questions, summarizing, empathy, affirmation, and assessment. The goal here is to engage the seminarian in authentic dialogue on issues relevant to his vocational call. It is interesting to note that Jesus displays each of these traits as he accompanies the two disciples on the road to Emmaus (Luke 24:13-53). Chapter four supplies a number of helpful templates that seminary formators can use when assessing the seminarian's suitability for the ministerial priesthood.

Taken as a whole, the book gives seminary formators an excellent tool for implementing the four pillars of priestly formation—the human, spiritual, intellectual, and pastoral—in a way that can be openly discussed, accurately assessed, and duly recorded. The book is highly focused and extremely practical. It will be a useful resource for seminary formators as they go about their work of preparing future priests for the life of missionary discipleship.

Fr. Dennis J. Billy, C.Ss.R.
Baltimore Province

CHAPTER ONE

Forming Seminary Formators in the Art of Accompaniment

Introduction

The Congregation for Sacred Education in *Directives Concerning the Preparation of Seminary Educators* (1994) indicates that the formator should "help the seminarian to know himself in depth, to accept himself with serenity and to correct himself and to mature, starting from real, not illusory, roots and from the 'heart' of his person".[1] The Congregation for Catholic Education in *Guidelines for the use of Psychology in the Admission and Formation of Candidates for the Priesthood* (2008) describes:

[T]he need for every formator to possess, in

---

[1] Congregation for Sacred Education, "Directives Concerning the Preparation of Seminary Educators" *(Origins* January 27, 1994, Volume 23, no.57).

due measure, the sensitivity and psychological preparation that will allow him, insofar as possible, to perceive the candidate's true motivations, to discern the barriers that stop him from integrating human and Christian maturity, and to pick up on any psychopathic disturbances present in the candidate...The formator must know how to evaluate the person in his totality, not forgetting the gradual nature of development. He must see the candidate's strong and weak points, as well as the level of awareness that the candidate has of his own problems. Lastly, the formator must discern the candidate's capacity for controlling his own behavior in responsibility and freedom.[2]

The Congregation for Clergy in the recent *Ratio Fundamentalis Institutionis Sacerdotalis* (December 2016) re-echoes that: "It is the task of every formator...to assist the seminarian in becoming aware of his condition, of the talents that he has received, and of his frailties, so that he can become ever more receptive to the action of grace."[3]

These are challenging obligations. Today's

---

[2] Congregation for Catholic Education, *Guidelines for the Use of Psychology in the Admission and Formation of Candidates for the Priesthood*, (June 29, 2008), no. 4.

[3] Congregation for Clergy, *Ratio Fundamentalis Institutionis Sacerdotalis* (December 8, 2016), no. 46.

generation of seminarians come with far less exposure to the Catholic faith than men decades ago. They have not come from a structured and predictable Catholic upbringing. Their weaknesses are less often due to adolescent struggles which are a normal process of growth and development. The secularization of the culture and advances in technology expose them to many more worldly ways than was possible before the advent of the Internet. Today's generation of young people are sexually "experienced". They know the world of addiction, especially pornography and online gaming with its violent and sexually promiscuous role playing themes. There is a growing population of young persons who come suffering with anxiety and depression. Seminarians also come older to the seminary with more deeply embedded daily habits that are not necessarily healthy or holy.

To form the seminarians of today, the *Ratio* states:

> Each formator should be possessed of human, spiritual, pastoral and professional abilities and resources, so as to *provide the right kind of accompaniment* that is balanced and respectful of the freedom and the conscience of the other person and that will help him in his human and spiritual growth.[4]

---

[4] Ibid, no. 49.

In order to be able to provide the **right kind of accompaniment**, the *Ratio* emphasizes that "those who are marked out to become formators need a specific preparation and generous dedication to the important task of formation."[5] Referencing Church documents on priestly formation and gleaning from the experience of dedicated seminary formators, this chapter will outline a specific preparation for the important task of forming formators in the art of accompaniment. I will consider five steps of accompaniment which address elements of what the *Ratio* refers to as the "right kind of accompaniment". Although intended for new seminary formators, these steps are useful for seasoned formators as well. I will also address employing psychological services to assist formators in the formation of seminarians as encouraged in Church documents.

The Road of Accompaniment[6]

STEP #1: Background Information as Groundwork for Accompaniment

The process of discerning authentic vocations to the priesthood requires that the formator come to a deeper understanding of who the seminarian is that he or she is accompanying. This process begins

---

[5] Ibid, no. 49.

[6] Cf. Template for The Road of Accompaniment on pp. 74-75.

even before the first meeting with the seminarian. In anticipation of this first meeting, the formator is to acquaint him or herself with what the man said about himself, how he lived his life to date, and what others said about him. This will be revealed as the formator reviews the elements of his seminary application. This will include the seminarian's autobiography, his statement of intent, his letters of recommendation and the summary of his psychological evaluation. Learning about the seminarian before beginning to meet with him offers a preliminary overview of the man.

A further comment regarding the psychological evaluation "as an integral part of the admission procedure" is drawn from the *Program for Priestly Formation* which states that a seminary applicant "should understand that the testing results will be shared with select seminary personnel in a way that permits a thorough review."[7] In 2008, the Congregation for Catholic Education in *Guidelines for the use of Psychology in the Admission and Formation of Candidates for the Priesthood*[8] stipulated:

> In a spirit of reciprocal trust and in co-operation with his own formator, the candidate can be invited freely to give his written consent so that the expert in the psychological sciences, who is bound by

---

[7] *PPF,* n. 52.

[8] Hereafter, *Guidelines.*

confidentiality, can communicate the results of the consultation to the formators indicated by the candidate himself. The formators will make use of any information thus acquired to sketch out a general picture of the candidate's personality, and to infer the appropriate indications for the candidate's further path of formation or for his admission to ordination.[9]

The Congregation for Catholic Education further clarified that "Inasmuch as it is the fruit of a particular gift of God, the vocation to the priesthood and its discernment lie outside the narrow competence of psychology."[10] The Congregation also requires that "particular care be taken so that the professional opinions expressed by the expert are exclusively accessible to those responsible for formation, with the precise and binding proscription against using it in any way other than for the discernment of a vocation and for the candidate's formation."[11]

Often, the formator is not offered any information about what is in the psychological evaluation regarding the man he or she is responsible to accompany in formation. The psychological evaluation is filed away after the admissions committee has reviewed it and not looked at again

---

[9] *Guidelines,* no. 13.
[10] Ibid, no. 5.
[11] Ibid, no. 13.

unless problems arise. Sometimes the rector gives the formators his thumbnail summary of what is contained in the psychological evaluation of each of the seminarians. Even in a small seminary, this can be a challenging task among the rector's many obligations. This approach, unwittingly, becomes a missed opportunity for the formator to make use of the information contained in the psychological evaluation regarding the seminarian's presenting level of affective maturity and where areas of affective growth can be supported and fostered. I recommend that seminaries develop a consent form that includes the seminary formator among the persons who have permission to view the result of a psychological evaluation explicitly for the purpose of assisting in the seminarian's vocational growth, development, and discernment.

Having obtained appropriate written consent, the formator should look for characteristics of maturity noted in the seminarian's psychological evaluation. For example, the seminarian's psycho-logical profile might indicate a man who is able to get along with others; who is collaborative, respon-sible, and service oriented; and who establishes and maintains relationships with appropriate boun-daries. Such characteristics suggest good prognosis for human formation. Characteristics of affective immaturity which suggest probable obstacles for affective growth include indications of entitlement, criticalness, isolative behaviors, a history of re-peated impaired judgment, repeated work and relationship difficulties, and conflicts with persons in roles of authority. The formator should seek to answer questions such as: Has the seminarian had psychotherapy? Have the therapy issues been satisfactorily addressed? Does he have multiple physical or medical concerns? Are there signs of addiction to the Internet? Substance abuse? Obviously, this is not a comprehensive list of what might be found in a psychological evaluation.

STEP #2: Clarifying Expectations of Accompaniment

It is important to establish parameters for the formation meetings. State the time, duration, frequency, and location of the formation meetings. It is also important that the formator explain the purpose and focus of the formation meetings keeping in mind that the goal of formation is to arrive at a vocational discernment, to shape the heart of a priest, and to form a missionary disciple of Christ. Remind the seminarian that the work of formation is dependent upon the Holy Spirit and the interior commitment he makes to exercise initiative in every aspect of his life. His free will engagement in the process of formation will lead him deeper each day into this interior commitment as one called to priesthood.

The formator is to let the seminarian know how best to contact him or her; that is, whether he or she prefers email, cell phone, or office phone. Persons vary in their preferences. The formator is to explain how best to reach him or her in the event of an emergency, or if the seminarian needs to cancel an appointment or desires to meet with the formator outside of the regularly scheduled meeting times.

The formator is to create an atmosphere of trust and safety in which it will be possible for the seminarian, in times of joy, as well as times of suffering, frustration, or dryness, to speak with the formator about his day-to-day vocational journey. Creating an atmosphere of trust is an essential element in the process of accompaniment. "The programme of formation should explore and outline the concrete ways in which this trust can be encouraged and safeguarded."[12] The relationship between formator and seminarian is also one with parameters of confidentiality. Respecting a seminarian's right of privacy is necessary, and careful management of confidential materials must be observed.[13]

The seminarian is to be reminded that the fruitfulness of the conversation during the forma-

---

[12] *Ratio*, no. 47.

[13] "This is especially true in the case of sharing confidential information with a team of formators, while at the same time ensuring that those charged with the candidate's growth and integration have clear and specific information they need so that they can help the candidate achieve the growth necessary to become a 'man of communion.'" Rev. Mark L. Bartchak, "Canonical Issues Concerning Confidentiality, Privacy Rights, Access to Data, and Record Keeping", *Seminary Journal*, vol. 14, n.1 (Spring 2008), p. 7. *PPF*, n. *93*

tion meeting depends on his praying and consulting the Holy Spirit regarding what should be discussed. There may be a long awaited insight or a question that remains, a situation that is troubling him, or a relationship that challenges him. He may be struggling with a passion or may be delighting in God's work in his life. The formator is to invite the seminarian to join him or her in attentive listening for what God seeks to reveal to him.[14,15] This will establish the tenor for the meetings as a sacred time during which the Holy Spirit plays a principal role in the life of the seminarian who is the primary agent of his own formation.

Fulfillment of the expectations that are clarified demonstrate the seminarian's earnest desire to cooperate in the process of formation. If a seminarian does not come prepared to his formation meeting, but instead focuses his discussion on, say, sports, the formator needs to point this out. If the seminarian frequently comes late for Morning Prayer, but shows up on time for breakfast, the formator has something to address. Clarifying expectations also communicates that the formator is available to the seminarian and desires to

---

[14] "During the process of formation...the seminarian is a 'mystery to himself'...On the one hand he is characterized by talents and gifts that have been moulded by grace; on the other he is marked by his limits and frailty." *Ratio,* no. 28.

[15] Formation is "understood as one unbroken missionary journey of discipleship...Its purpose is to form a priestly heart." *Ratio,* no. 54, 55.

support him in his formation process. The formator also offers prayers and sacrifice for the seminarian in his charge. He or she is willing and able to appropriately affirm the seminarian with whom he or she is working, and when necessary to challenge him.

STEP # 3: Discovering God's Design through the Review of Life in Accompaniment

Having clarified expectations, the formator then moves to the Review of Life. In Step #1, the formator read before the first meeting the background on the seminarian with whom he or she will be working. While background history is helpful, it is important that this background not become the total assessment of the seminarian.

The formator needs to come to know the man himself, that is, learn about his life history as articulated directly from him in the formation meetings. The purpose of the dialogue concerning his life history is to explore together God's design for the seminarian. The *Ratio* emphasizes the importance of the Review of Life to develop an individualized plan of formation. "In order for this training to be fruitful, it is important that every seminarian be aware of his own life history, and be ready to share it with his formators."[16] One of the goals of seminary formation is to help the seminarian articulate an honest understanding of

---

[16] *Ratio*, no. 94.

himself, with his complex make-up, weaknesses and potentialities toward a priestly identity. The *PPF* states:

> Just as the seminary recognizes that the positive qualities of a seminarian's prior formation can both indicate a vocation and provide a solid foundation for further growth, it should also address possible deficiencies in the candidate's earlier formation and find means to address them.[17]

To be formative, accompaniment must include, right from the beginning, recognizing through the lens of faith, the deeper meanings of certain events in the seminarian's life, i.e., how God was present in an experience the seminarian had, although it may not have been apparent to him at the time. Looking at what happened through the lens of faith is always a moment of grace that offers an opportunity to ponder how our past experiences are part of God's unfolding design for our salvation. We have all had the experience that certain past events make sense only in the context of faith. This step of seeking a deeper understanding of the events of the seminarian's salvation history continues throughout the process of accompaniment.

---

[17] *PPF*, n.88.

Step #4: Fostering Affective Growth and Development in Accompaniment

Vocational accompaniment offers the seminarian a means to gradually grow in self-knowledge. With what has been gleaned over the course of formation meetings, the formator is to help the seminarian acquire an accurate understanding of himself and thus grow in personal freedom. A more comprehensive understanding of the seminarian's life history will be key in order to identify together areas where he could grow in self-knowledge and address deficiencies in his affective level of functioning. Appropriate self-disclosure and a cultivated capacity for self-reflection and accountability are among the requisite habits and skills of a man in seminary formation.[18] The *Ratio* encourages the seminarian to share his life history as part of his formation journey: "This sharing would include especially his experience of childhood and adolescence, [and] the influence that his family and his relatives have exercised upon him."[19]

Consider a seminarian who had a difficult relationship with his father. The seminarian may project unresolved hurts from his past experiences with his father onto persons in authority with whom he relates in the present. Psychological projection involves unconsciously attributing un-

---

[18] Ibid, n. 93.
[19] *Ratio*, no. 94.

desirable feelings or emotions onto someone else, rather than admitting to or dealing with the unwanted feelings. The seminarian may react with fear and aggression toward his formator, superiors, and certain parishioners, for example, if they remind him of his difficult relationship with his father. He would benefit greatly from the formator's assistance in bringing to awareness the emotional residue of his past and the impact that this is having on present relationships. Unaddressed projections will hinder the seminarian's ability to grow in freedom and make the choices formation requires.

The formator is to guide the seminarian to open himself to a continuum of transformations from within his own personal history. This will at times include personal mentoring:

> They [the formators] observe seminarians and assist them to grow humanly by offering them feedback about their general demeanor, their relational capacities and styles, their maturity, their capacity to assume the role of a public person and leader in a community, and their appropriation of the human virtues that make them "men of communion." These same formators may, on occasion, teach the ways of human development and even offer some personal mentoring or, at times, coaching. More generally, they offer encouragement, support, and challenge along the forma-

tional path.[20]

As part of addressing affective growth and development of seminarians, a formator with whom I worked addressed table manners and personal hygiene with his men. Some men come from families in which they did not have sit down meals. This formator would say in jest, "This is Mr. Knife and this is Mrs. Fork and this is how you engage them when you are at table". If a seminarian looked unkempt, the formator gave him immediate feedback. If the man was not showering regularly, he reminded the seminarian that he is being formed to be a public person. If the seminarian came down for breakfast unshaven, and was not trying to grow a beard, the formator waited until the seminarian had a hot plate of food and then told him to go shave and then return to eat his breakfast. "They quickly get the point and they change," remarked this formator. Addressing areas of human formation in a timely fashion also communicates that the formator is invested in the seminarian's human formation and desires that he grow in self-discipline. Seminaries are not looking for perfect candidates, but there are basic expectations for men called to priesthood.

In the process of fostering affective growth, the formator will want to remind the seminarian that the goal of formation is to be configured to Christ as

---

[20] *PPF,* no. 80.

a man of communion.[21] The formator will emphasize that to be configured to Christ cannot be completed without regular and faithful encounters with Christ in prayer. That prayer, joined to the seminarian's cooperation with human and spiritual formation, aided by grace, leads him to respond to God, who speaks to his heart from the deepest core of his personality. It took the disciples time to take on the heart and mind of Christ. Each stage of formation must directly impact the maturation process. Such an awareness invites the seminarian to make deliberate changes when necessary. The formator is to guide the seminarian to discern where conversion is gradually evolving, is very slow in evolving, or not taking place. The formator is to guide the seminarian in examining and challenging his attitudes and behaviors. Some attitudes he keeps and fosters. Others he needs to grow into.

Step #5: Discerning whether the Seminarian is Assuming the Sentiments of Christ[22] Required for Ministerial Priesthood

The process of accompanying a seminarian takes place in a variety of settings and through multiple shared experiences of formation within the community life of the seminary. These are hopefully integrated through relationships with vocation directors, faculty formators, peers, and bishops.

---

[21] Ibid, no. 112.
[22] *Ratio*, no. 41.

The community life of the seminary provides many good opportunities for formation, offering an environment in which the formation team may assess seminarians and verify, in the context of daily living, a seminarian's capacity for healthy "give-and-take" in relationships. For example, formators are able to identify a seminarian's ability to develop healthy interpersonal boundaries, transcend his personal points of view and personal preferences, achieve a deepening self-awareness and spiritual life, analyze and communicate difficulties, demonstrate self-sacrifice, and relate comfortably with all types of people. The com-munity life of the seminary also offers the opportunity for the formation team to observe the quality of the seminarian's relationships with persons in roles of authority. Obedience and respect are necessary, as are honesty, integrity, and candor. These qualities all reflect a seminarian's overall level of maturity.

Pastoral assignments and internships provide added opportunities in which to assess the suitability of a seminarian. Some dioceses or seminaries offer a spirituality year. Does the seminarian bear witness to the compassionate presence of Jesus Christ in his life? Does he contribute to drawing parishioners closer to God by his presence? Is he responsible in his pastoral assignment? Does he exhibit the potential for pastoral charity? What is the caliber of his relationships with his own family and others?

Opportunities for self-evaluation are also important. How does the seminarian's self-image compare with the image depicted by his formators, non-formation staff members, auxiliary personnel (e.g. secretarial staff, maintenance personnel) and persons to whom he ministers? Peer evaluations also provide additional information.

Formators need to be adequately prepared to carry out a discernment that, fully respecting the Church's doctrine on priestly vocation, allows for a reasonably sure decision as to whether the seminarian should be advanced in formation.[23] Conversely, respecting a seminarian's right of privacy is necessary, and careful management of confidential materials must be observed. "This is especially true in the case of sharing confidential information with a team of formators, while at the same time ensuring that those charged with the candidate's growth and integration have the clear and specific information they need so that they can help the candidate achieve the growth necessary to become a 'man of communion.'"[24]

There are times when it is discovered that the seminarian has psychological wounds that are outside the realm of the formator's competency to address. It is important to refer him to a professional in such situations, especially if these areas of woundedness can be healed and free the seminarian to embrace a vocation to priesthood.

---

[23] *Guidelines,* no. 3.

[24] Rev. Mark L. Bartchak, "Canonical Issues Concerning Confidentiality, Privacy Rights, Access to Data, and Record Keeping", *Seminary Journal,* vol. 14, n.1, (Spring 2008), p. 7.

While some seminarians flourish and grow in their vocation, other seminarians exhibit a variety of struggles. For example, seminarians may demonstrate a reduction of energy and enthusiasm for the spiritual life and ministry, a limited ability to witness to the person of Jesus Christ, psychosexual struggles, and a diminished capacity to remain faithful in a lifelong commitment. To provide the right kind of accompaniment, the formator must understand, as best as is possible, a seminarian's level of human functioning. Is the seminarian's psychological woundedness hindering his capacity to engage in and benefit from priestly formation? Is he aware of his areas of emotional underdevelopment? Is he willing to address areas of emotional immaturity contributing to relational deficiencies? Can these weaknesses be addressed through dialogue with formators? Would psychotherapy be helpful? What kinds of deficiencies mitigate against the viability of a vocation?

There are circumstances when the effects of wounds will not be sufficiently alleviated with therapy. Such a case will hinder the man from reaching the affective maturity necessary for priestly ministry. If more psychological work is being done than human or spiritual formation, the man should not be advanced in formation. This does not mean he is not loved by God, but he may not have a priestly vocation. "While psychology and the human sciences can be resources for human formation, they are not the same as human formation."[25] The seminarian may have had a powerful conversion to the Catholic faith or a reversion back to the faith. This may not indicate a vocation to priesthood. Maybe his conversion was his coping mechanism.

If the formator is working harder than the seminarian or therapeutic issues become overwhelming, it is an injustice to keep the man in the seminary. A seminarian may be the most intellectual and prayerful candidate, but if human formation is not taking place, the man will be less effective as a priest than he could be. Therapy is not human formation. A seminary is not a psychotherapy center. Seminaries provide tremendous opportunities for human development, but they cannot supply everything. Be honest with the candidates who come to your seminary. Remember, the "squeaky wheel" in the seminary, if ordained, becomes the "squeaky wheel" in the parish with parishioners. It might have been more charitable to discontinue formation during his first year. This can be the greatest difficulty for formators. If a seminarian is there for three years and he is still not who the formation team thinks he should be, he needs to be dismissed from the seminary for his sake and the sake of the Church.

The *Program for Priestly Formation* in no. 105 states:

Seminarians in need of long-term therapy

---

[25] *PPF,* no. 105.

should avail themselves of such assistance before entering the seminary, or should leave the program until the therapy has been completed. If such a departure be indicated, there should be no expectation of automatic readmission. A candidate should not be considered for advancement to Holy Orders if he is engaged in long-term psychological therapy. Issues being addressed in counseling should be satisfactorily settled prior to the call to Holy Orders.

The formator will look for signs that manifest progress in the process of being configured to Christ. Key in looking for these signs is what motivates the seminarian to do what he does and in what manner he does what he does. Is he motivated by Christ and love for the Church? Are there signs of his willingness to give himself to others, even in small ways? Does he regard and treat each person with respect and dignity? Does he exhibit charity? Does he encounter others in their real needs, especially the poor, elderly, and difficult? Is he patient in difficult situations? Does he readily forgive? Does he seek forgiveness? Does he lead persons with a pastoral sensitivity to their sufferings and joys? Is he humble in carrying out tasks assigned to him? Does he have a simple lifestyle? Does he accept and endure suffering as a participation in the redemptive work of Christ? Love for Christ and the Church motivates a fraternal attitude toward all persons. One configured to Christ engenders in another a profound experience of belonging. The formator is responsible for discerning whether the seminarian is embracing and benefiting from formation.

Closing recommendations

To promote the right kind of accompaniment, I offer the following recommendations which provide specific structures and procedures for seminarians, bishops, religious superiors, vocation directors, and seminary personnel for more effective collaboration amongst the formation team members.

☐ Develop a consent form to obtain written permission from each seminary candidate for access to the admission psychiatric/psychological evaluation. Also:

- Specify the formation team members who may have access to the evaluation
- Indicate that use of the evaluation be for the explicit purpose of the seminarian's vocational growth, development, and discernment

☐ Establish protocols for the access and use of psychiatric and psychological evaluations when a seminarian has undergone a course of therapy; determine a period of retention of records; and establish a policy for destruction of those records by the dioceses, religious communities, and seminaries

☐ Establish similar retention protocols for records kept by formators

Conclusion

I will conclude by taking a passage from the Gospel of John that illustrates the process of accompaniment in formation. Consider the actions of Jesus as he speaks to the woman at the well[26] and the similarities to the process of accompaniment. The woman encounters Jesus at the well. He poses questions to her. She is guarded with her answers. He speaks the truth in love to her. He does not condemn her. The Samaritan woman receives the truth about herself from Jesus because she experiences His love. She can now speak freely. She knows herself loved and accepted despite her human frailties. As she begins to know her true self through the experience of Christ's merciful love, she is freed to joyfully proclaim the good news. In the ordinary action of a formation meeting, there is something extraordinary taking place.[27]

---

[26] John 4: 5 -42.

[27] An earlier draft of this paper was presented for the Seminary Formation Council Certificate Program for seminary formators in June, 2017. I am grateful for suggested revisions to this chapter from the following

persons: Sister Mary Kathleen Ronan, RSM, PhD, Sister Mary Prudence Allen, RSM, PhD, Sister Mary Cora Uryase, RSM, PhD and Rev. Msgr. Thomas Caserta, DMin.

CHAPTER TWO

Markers of Human Maturation in Seminary Formation: Becoming a Gift for Others[28]

The 2008 document from the Congregation for Catholic Education, *Guidelines for the Use of Psychology in the Admission and Formation of Seminarians for the Priesthood* and the recent document from the Congregation for Clergy the *Ratio Fundamentalis Institutionis Sacerdotalis* highlight the duty of bishops and formators to discern the suitability of seminarians for ordained priestly ministry.[29] Formators must know how to

---

[28] Cf. Template for Markers of Human Maturation in Seminary Formation: Becoming a Gift for Others on pp. 75-86.

[29] Congregation for Catholic Education, *Guidelines for the Use of Psychology in the Admission and Formation of Seminarians for the Priesthood* (October, 2008), no.2. Congregation for the Clergy, *Ratio Fundamentalis Institutionis Sacerdotalis* (December 8, 2016), no. 44, 46.

evaluate a man in his totality.[30] Cited among the virtues and abilities required in a priest are a positive and stable sense of his masculine identity, the capacity to form mature relationships, a solid sense of belonging, self-knowledge, the capacity for self-correction, the ability for trust and loyalty, and the courage to stay faithful to decisions made before God.[31]

A seminarian does not automatically possess these virtues and abilities upon acceptance to the seminary. Maturation gradually occurs through the integration of human, spiritual, intellectual, and pastoral dimensions of formation joined with the seminarian's continued cooperation with the work of divine grace.[32] The *Program for Priestly Formation* states: "Since formation assumes that a seminarian will be growing both in God's grace and in his free human response to that grace it is important that there be a process to note the markers of that growth."[33]

This chapter is intended to assist formators in that responsibility. Determining the level of affective maturity of a seminarian and his potential for human development requires that formators ask

---

[30] *Guidelines*, no.4.

[31] *Guidelines*, no.2. *Ratio* no. 41.

[32] Committee on Priestly Formation of the United States Conference of Catholic Bishops, *Program of Priestly Formation*, fifth edition. (Washington, D.C.: United States Conference of Catholic Bishops, September, 2006), no. 272.

[33] *Ibid,* no. 272.

suitable questions and make prudential observations. A seminarian may be more developed in one area than another. A composite view is necessary to determine the level of maturation of each seminarian and to discern the seminarian's suitability for priestly formation and for diaconal and priestly ordination when that time comes.

Markers of human maturation reflect characteristics that indicate increasing personal and interpersonal affective development. Major theories of psychiatry and psychology depict a sequential process in human personality development. There are theoretical differences in the human maturational models of Freud, Jung, Erikson, and Maslow, for example, but all models contain similar characteristics that indicate increasing personal and interpersonal integration.[34] A similar sequential process of human becoming is expressed by Saint John Paul II in *The Acting Person*.[35]

There are six interrelated markers that are common to all major theories of human development. The following terms will be used to characterize them: self-knowledge, self-direction, self-control, self-discipline, self-governance, and spiritual fatherhood. They are listed in ascending order of affective maturity. Since personal growth and

---

[34] Benjamin James Sadock, M.D. and Virginia Alcott Sadock, M.D., *Kaplan and Sadock's Synopsis of Psychiatry*, ninth edition (Philadelphia: Lippincott Williams and Wilkins, 2003), p. 18-21, 199-216.

[35] John Paul II, *The Acting Person* (Boston: D. Reidel Publishing Company, 1979).

development does not take place in discretely delineated stages, you will note overlap in the markers. Each marker has a sampling of questions to guide bishops, vocation directors, and seminary formators in their evaluation of a seminarian's level of affective maturity. Placing check marks beside the questions within each marker of affective maturity or immaturity will offer formators a focus for a written narrative of a seminarian's level of affective functioning as well as specific examples of where the seminarian has room to grow. Most seminaries recommend an annual assessment of each seminarian.

Self-Awareness to Self-Knowledge

The first maturational marker is self-knowledge. This entails the capacity to understand one's thoughts and feelings and how these relate to behavior. This provides the basis for capacities to give and receive from others without excessive dependence or defensiveness.[36] Self-knowledge allows one to rely on other people with a sense of trust as well as a sense of self-reliance and self-trust.

A seminarian who understands his thoughts and feelings and how they relate to behavior is self-reliant yet at the same time able to rely on and entrust himself to others.

---

[36] Sadock and Sadock, p. 212.

Questions to assess whether a seminarian is exhibiting this maturational marker:

☐ Does he exhibit:

- The ability to acknowledge his feelings?

- Emotional stability?

- A desire to gain a more complete and accurate knowledge of his motivations?

- Appropriate self-disclosure?

☐ Does he manifest a willingness to admit to mistakes?

☐ Is he appropriately self-reliant with a capacity to trust himself yet at the same time able to rely on and entrust himself to others?

A seminarian who is limited in his ability to reflect upon his emotions and thoughts and how they relate to his behaviors demonstrates tendencies toward emotional turmoil and anxiety. He may be a "people-pleaser" who can feel alienated from others due to his anxiety or anger about "not measuring up." He may try to "make up" for what is lacking in his sense of self by excessive ingratiating behaviors.

He may also blame others for his relational difficulties without insight or desire to grow in self-knowledge.

Questions to assess whether a seminarian exhibits limited self-knowledge:

☐ Are the seminarian's relationships needy and emotionally charged?

☐ Do his relationships terminate in frustration because of his neediness or emotional outbursts?

☐ Does he withdraw when emotionally conflicted?

☐ Does he exhibit excessive ingratiating behaviors?

☐ Does he give evidence of feeling undervalued?

☐ Does he give evidence of being self-focused?

For example:

• Is he mostly about me, my, and mine?

- Is he unaware of what is going on around him?

☐ Does he frequently avoid acknowledging personal faults?

☐ Does he prefer to have others make decisions for him so as to avoid responsibility?

Self-Direction

Self-direction is the basis for evolving personal autonomy without undo self-doubt or ambivalence. Self-direction is necessary for cooperation in which there is neither excessive submissiveness nor willfulness.[37]

A seminarian who is mature in his interactions is motivated to prevent the buildup of frustration from emotionally conflicted situations. He does not require that he get his own way in order to be successful. He has the capacity to engage in interdependent activities with peers and persons in authority. His interactive style often elicits cooperation from others. People who exude a strong personal presence do not intimidate the mature seminarian. He is able to differ with other people without dismissing those with whom he disagrees. He is empathic but does not assume others' feelings

---

[37] Ibid. p. 213.

and behaviors.

Questions to assess whether a seminarian exhibits appropriate self-direction:

☐ Is he able to receive criticism with docility and address it?

☐ Does he exhibit appropriate initiative?

☐ Can he accept a difficult situation and function within it?

☐ Has he achieved the capacity to differ with others' opinions without dismissing those with whom he disagrees?

☐ Is he comfortable in the presence of authority persons without antagonism or withdrawal from relationship?

A seminarian struggling with limited self-direction can be impulsive or rigid. He has difficulty making everyday decisions. As a consequence of his self-doubt, he assumes an ambivalent posture of suspicious vigilance to guard against being hurt by others. He may be excessively compliant, exhibiting a lack of personal autonomy and initiative. He may conform, yet internally he is filled with rebellion and critical judgment.

Questions to assess whether a seminarian exhibits limited self-direction:

☐ Does he prefer to have others make decisions for him?

☐ Does he demonstrate excessive compliance?

☐ Is he rigid and lacking a capacity for flexibility in interactions?

☐ Does he seek the attention of authority persons to build up his self-worth?

☐ Does he use others for what they can do for him?

☐ Does he exhibit a lack of personal autonomy and initiative?

☐ Does he exhibit ambivalence and self-doubt?

☐ Does he lack a capacity to cooperate with others?

☐ Is he frequently in conflict with authority persons?

Self-Control

Self-control entails establishing the motivation for necessary change, setting clear goals, and monitoring behaviors toward that goal. This capacity underlies all kinds of achievements. Self-control provides a healthy sense of pride and self-competence derived from performance.[38]

A seminarian with self-control is able to delay gratification for a future good. He has the capacity to realistically anticipate and plan for future potential difficulties. He derives a healthy sense of pride and self-competence from his work. A seminarian who exhibits appropriate self-control prefers to work with others and is viewed by his peers as a "team player." He is open to others' ideas and seeks harmony while appreciating diversity.

Questions to assess whether a seminarian exhibits self-control:

☐ Does the seminarian exercise responsible stewardship in his use of time and resources?

☐ Does he exhibit a healthy sense of pride and self-competence from his work?

---

[38] Ibid. p. 213.

☐ Is he able to delay gratification for a future or greater good?

☐ Does he have a capacity for balancing harmony and diversity?

☐ Does he experience a heightened sense of fulfillment through collaboration with others in ministry?

☐ Does he encourage those with whom he is working to search for the good in others' ideas?

Inferiority and inadequacy are common experiences for a seminarian who struggles with self-control. He does not feel competent or valued in his efforts and is critical of others and himself. He lacks joy in authentic self-giving. Such a seminarian needs to "prove" his adequacy. This can lead to "burn out," as he realizes increased labor does not substitute for his impaired self-esteem. A seminarian who experiences these limitations demands frequent affirmation.

Questions to assess whether a seminarian exhibits limited self-control:

☐ Does he exhibit strong emotional reactions when someone "crosses" him?

☐ Does he feel incompetent or undervalued?

☐ Is he excessively critical of others or himself?

☐ Does he lack a sense of joy in authentic self-giving?

☐ Is he bothered by feelings of inferiority and inadequacy?

☐ Does he exhibit frequent negative murmuring or sarcasm?

☐ Does he exhibit apathy or "burnout" when his work performance does not compensate for his low self-esteem?

☐ Does he lack the capacity for appropriate delayed gratification?

Self-Discipline

Self-discipline requires motivation to achieve core values or habits. This necessitates effectively aligning thoughts and behaviors toward achieving those core values or habits. This process requires change and adaptation, gradually transforming how one sees oneself and how one interacts with others in various circumstances. Focused effort at living one's life also enhances self-confidence through the experience of greater self-control in executing tasks directed toward specific goals.[39]

A seminarian who exhibits balanced self-discipline has a sufficiently developed self-concept, is able to acknowledge his strengths and weaknesses, and demonstrates realistic problem solving skills. He has the capacity to form relationships in a mature manner; he is not preoccupied with his own needs.

Questions to assess whether a seminarian exhibits self-discipline:

☐ Does he exhibit appropriate interpersonal boundaries?

☐ Does he relate respectfully to women and men?

☐ Does he exercise discretion in his use of technology and choices of entertainment?

☐ Does he make choices that enable him to refrain from addictive behaviors?

(For example, regarding his use of alcohol and use of the Internet)

---

[39] Ibid. p. 214.

☐ Does he demonstrate realistic problem solving skills?

A seminarian who exhibits limited self-discipline may seek self-gratifying behaviors, such as overeating, alcohol abuse, or sexual activity, as a means to address or avoid stress, loneliness, or frustration. He is unsure of himself and relies on the role he plays to define his value and sense of personal security. Struggling to "find" himself, he may also be envious of others. His envy can flare into aggressive impulses or patterns of isolation.

Questions to assess whether a seminarian exhibits limited self-discipline:

☐ Does he have enmeshed relationships with poor interpersonal boundaries?

☐ Does he have more acquaintances than friendships?

☐ Does the seminarian rely heavily on the role he plays to define his sense of personal adequacy and security?

☐ Does he have to "prove" his adequacy by his performance?

☐ Does he engage in pleasurable excesses?

Self-Governance

A person who exhibits self-governance has integrated and consolidated previous attainments and is establishing decisive patterns for future adaptive functioning.[40] That is, he not only takes responsibility for his actions but has taken responsibility for the quality of his actions.[41] He is able to form relationships that are responsible, respectful, and marked by integrity. He does not focus on his emotional turmoil but instead invests his energy in problem-solving or bringing a situation to a positive conclusion. In stressful situations, he reflects on his own thoughts, feelings, and behaviors in order to better understand himself and other people's reactions to him. He has the ability to sustain loyalties freely pledged in spite of inevitable contradictions. The capacity for fidelity is the cornerstone for overall human stability.

A seminarian who exhibits self-governance takes responsibility for the quality of his actions. A seminarian who demonstrates a capacity for healthy friendship is able to respond to the challenges of relationship as a normal part of human bonding. At the same time, he is comfortable with solitude.

---

[40] Ibid. p. 214.

[41] John Paul II, *The Acting Person* (Boston: D. Reidel Publishing Company, 1979), p. 107.

Self-governance is the quality that directs our free acts to the existential ends that God places in our nature, so that we can live a truly human life as *imago Dei*.42 With such personal integration, the acting person manifests fidelity to transcendental truths. He embraces suffering in his own life and is empathic with people who are suffering. He demonstrates a capacity for fidelity to his faith and the courage to make decisions according to his faith.

Questions to assess whether a seminarian exhibits self-governance:

☐ Does he demonstrate sound prudential judgment in his choices?

☐ Is he able to form relationships that are responsible, respectful, and marked by integrity?

☐ Does he manifest an ability to forgive others and seek forgiveness for personal shortcomings?

☐ Does he understand suffering in his own life and respond accordingly?

☐ Does he show compassion to those who are suffering?

---

42 Ibid. p. 106-108.

☐ Does he exhibit faithful perseverance in fulfilling commitments?

☐ Is he faithful to the vocation with which he is identifying?

☐ Does he address self-denial, loneliness, and celibacy in a mature manner that also serve to enrich his life?

A seminarian who is limited in self-governance has difficulty controlling his own actions and responses. The choices he makes are not linked to any particular hierarchy of ends. He allows his emotions, his mere likes and dislikes, to control the actions he takes. He excuses himself from responsibilities when in situations that make him uncomfortable. He has a poor self-image. He tends to have difficulty setting aside his own needs. He consequently has a limited sense of the needs of others. He is more focused on being viewed as "good" rather than striving to grow in virtue. He alternates between idolizing certain individuals when they satisfy his needs and disliking persons who do not meet his needs. When contradictions in values or morals present themselves, he lacks fidelity and the courage necessary to make decisions in accord with the Catholic Church to which he is called to bear witness.

Questions to assess whether a seminarian exhibits limited self-governance:

☐ Does he function poorly in a stressful or delicate situation?

☐ Does he fail to fulfill commitments he has made?

☐ Are his interpersonal relationships characterized by superficiality?

☐ Does he demonstrate a limited sensitivity to the sufferings of others?

☐ Is he ambivalent about his sexual orientation, moral values, or commitments?

☐ Is celibacy a burden for him?

☐ Does he lack a capacity for fidelity to the teachings of the Catholic Church?

Spiritual Fatherhood

Saint John Paul II in *Pastores Dabo Vobis* speaks of the priest as one called to make a gift-of-self in likeness to Christ:

The gift of self has no limits, marked as it is by the same apostolic and missionary zeal of Christ, the good shepherd, who said: "And I have other sheep that are not of this fold; I must bring them also, and they will heed my voice. So there shall be one flock, one shepherd" (Jn. 10:16).[43]

A seminarian who demonstrates a capacity for spiritual fatherhood has a disposition to minister to the needs of others. He is personally enriched by his self-gift. He has primary concern for the welfare and enrichment of others. He does not shrink from self-sacrifice.

Questions to assess a seminarian's disposition for spiritual fatherhood:

☐ Does he manifest a "strong, lively, personal love" of Jesus Christ?

☐ Does he exhibit the capacity to mentor?

☐ Is he an instrument directing others to God?

☐ Does he exhibit a disposition for service?

---

[43] John Paul II, Post Synodal Apostolic Exhortation, *Pastores Dabo Vobis* (March 25, 1992), no. 23.

☐ Is he enriched by his service?

☐ Is he striving for conversion from attitudes contrary to pastoral charity?

☐ Does he consistently exhibit a capacity for self-sacrifice trusting in God?

☐ Does he display the capacity to renounce the goods of marriage for spiritual fatherhood?

A seminarian who has a limited disposition for spiritual fatherhood struggles with generosity. He seeks self-aggrandizement, undue recognition, and relationships that provide him with status or human respect. In short, a seminarian who does not demonstrate qualities of spiritual fatherhood will be limited in a capacity for self-sacrifice and altruism.

Questions to assess a seminarian who has a limited disposition for spiritual fatherhood:

☐ Does his love for himself surpass his love for others?

☐ Does he prefer "privileged" work?

☐ Does he manifest a need to be "successful"

in ministry?

☐ Does he use relationships with others for self-aggrandizement?

☐ Does he manifest inappropriate possessiveness of his gifts?

☐ Is he insensitive to what is going on around him?

☐ Does he lack a capacity to be self-sacrificing and altruistic?

Narrative Assessment

After placing a check mark beside each question where a seminarian exhibits observable behaviors related to a marker of maturation, the next task is to write a narrative assessment. The formator is to write specific examples of the traits observed in a particular seminarian. These include the seminarian's presently noted strengths and specific examples of where he has room to grow. It is also important to make practical recommendations regarding ways a seminarian can address areas where affective growth is necessary. An example is provided below.

Seminarian:
Year in Formation:
Formator:
Date:

- What are the seminarian's strengths presently in his formation process? Give specific examples as reflected in significant markers of human maturation.

- Where does he have room to grow? Give specific examples as reflected in significant markers of human maturation.

- List practical recommendations to address vocational growth and development.

Conclusion

By assessing the level of affective maturity, the Church provides seminarians encouragement to continue their formation and wisdom to identify ways in which their formation may take deeper root.[44] It is through receptivity to God's grace, joined to the exercise of human freedom, whereby one grows to become most fully oneself. It will be important to ascertain if the seminarian is growing both in God's grace and in his free human response

---

[44] *PPF*, no. 272.

to that grace.

Saint John Paul II, in addressing the formation of seminarians for the priesthood, describes that it is only when one becomes a gift for others that one most fully becomes oneself:

> Human maturity, and in particular affective maturity, requires a clear and strong training in freedom which expresses itself in convinced and heartfelt obedience to the "truth" of one's own being, to the "meaning" of one's own existence, that is to the "sincere gift of self" as the way and fundamental content of the authentic realization of the self.[45]

The *Ratio* re-echoes this necessary pastoral sentiment:

> Thus, by growing in charity, the future priest must seek to develop a balanced and mature capacity to enter into relationship with his neighbor. Indeed, he is called above all to a basic human and spiritual serenity that, by overcoming every form of self-promotion or emotional dependency, allows him to be a man of communion, of mission and of dialogue. In contemplating the Lord, who offered His life for others, he will be

---

[45] *PDV,* no. 44.

able to give himself generously and with self-sacrifice for God's people.[46]

May the vineyard of the Lord be rich with such self-sacrificing priests.

---

[46] *Ratio,* no.41.

CHAPTER THREE

Communication Skills for Formative Dialogue Directed toward Missionary Discipleship[47]

This chapter will consider various skills needed for a formative dialogue between a seminarian and formator. These skills include: reflective listening, open-ended questions, summarizing, empathy, affirmation, and assessment. In the context of a conversation, a particular communication skill readily opens to the use of another skill. You will therefore note overlap in the description of each skill.

Reflective listening

An essential element in the process of accompaniment in formation is listening. Admittedly, we

---

[47] Cf. Template for Communication Skills for Formative Dialogue Directed Toward Missionary Discipleship on pp. 87-92.

live in an age which is challenged by the deluge of electronic modes of communication. This has led to giving limited and brief attention to written messages and diminished attention to spoken messages. Reflective listening is a strategy of communication involving two steps. First, the formator seeks to understand what the seminarian meant by what he said. Second, the formator seeks to confirm the accuracy of what he understood.

Pope Francis, in his 50th World Day Communication Message of January 24, 2016, entitled *Communication and Mercy* reminds us that attentive listening is a grace that needs to be sought.

> Listening is never easy...Listening means paying attention, wanting to understand, to value, to respect and to ponder what the other person says. It involves a sort of martyrdom or self-sacrifice....Knowing how to listen is an immense grace, it is a gift which we need to ask for and then make every effort to practice.

Listening seems like easy work. For those who engage in reflective listening, it is arduous work. It is the work of building a rapport between the seminarian and the formator.

Reflective listening is a sacred encounter where the intersection of God's grace and human communication is found. This is aptly described by Pope Francis in *Communication and Mercy:*

Communication,...open[s] up broader horizons...[between] people. This is a gift of God which involves a great responsibility. I like to refer to this power of communication as 'closeness'. The encounter between communication and mercy will be fruitful to the degree that it generates a closeness which cares, comforts, heals, accompanies and celebrates.

In such an encounter, the seminarian perceives that his formator has a genuine desire to understand him. One of the most common obstacles to reflective listening occurs when the formator assumes he knows what the seminarian means without further exploration. For example, if the formator hears the seminarian say, "I wish I was more outgoing", and does not explore this statement more fully, he may miss what the seminarian intended. The seminarian may be thinking: "I feel lonely and I want to have more friends"; "I get very nervous when I have to speak to a group of people"; "I should spend more time getting to know people"; or "I can't think of anything to say when I am with people".

Skillful use of reflective listening will help the formator gain a greater understanding of the seminarian. For example, what interests, excites, or energizes him. He may uncover as well what frustrates him, what makes him anxious and what challenges him. By reflective listening, the formator may come to note tension in the seminarian's description of a relationship. The formator may hear that the seminarian seems overly attached to someone. If the seminarian speaks frequently of missing what he did before he entered seminary, the formator may want to explore this further.

Attention to nonverbal communication is another aspect of reflective listening. Some examples of this are the tone of voice, facial expression, and body movements. Studies have shown that 93% of communication is nonverbal. Linguists tell us that 7% is communicated with words, 55% is communicated with body movements and facial expressions, and 38% is communicated with voice tone, modulation and pauses.

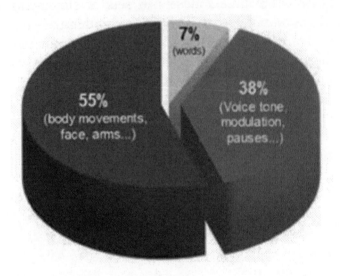

This being the case, if the formator is to gain a more complete view of the seminarian, then nonverbal communication is very important. Millennials, that is persons born between 1981 and 2000, are accustomed to sharing more online than face-to-face. They can spend as much time socializing with friends virtually present to them on Facebook, Twitter, Instagram, etc., as with those persons actually present to them. This has led to a diminished ability in millennials to recognize and understand their own nonverbal communication, as well as that of others. The formator must be attentive to the fact that 93% of his or her <u>own</u> communication is also nonverbal.

The tone of voice is an especially powerful nonverbal means of communicating understanding or of seeking further clarification. Consider the difference between these two sets of statements where voice inflection changes the meaning of what is communicated. "You were feeling uncomfortable?" or "You were feeling uncomfortable." Another example, "You don't think this is a concern?" or "You don't think this is a concern." In English, the voice tone typically goes up at the end of a question, but generally goes down at the end of a statement to communicate understanding. The differences are subtle but real.

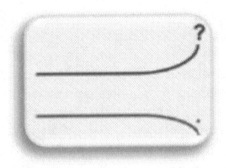

Reflective listening is an important skill. It communicates that the formator is attentively listening with a desire to understand what the seminarian is saying. The formator's desire to understand contributes to the seminarian's experience of the formator's care for him. This human encounter, where understanding and care is communicated by the formator, fosters trust in the seminarian and a willingness for appropriate transparency.[48]

Open-ended questions

The second communication skill I will address is the use of open-ended questions. Open-ended questions are "door openers" that invite the seminarian to describe an experience in greater detail. Such questions help the formator under-stand the seminarian's point of view and provide for a richer and deeper conversation. Asking open-ended ques-

---

[48] Congregation for Clergy, *Ratio Fundamentalis Institutionis Sacerdotalis* (December 8, 2016), no. 45.

tions helps the formator avoid making premature judgments. Its opposite, a closed-ended question, can be answered by a simple "yes" or "no".

Jesus often used open-ended questions to invite those listening into a deeper conversation with Him. Consider how Jesus does this on the "Walk to Emmaus":

> That very day two of them were going to a village named Emmaus, about seven miles from Jerusalem, and talking with each other about all these things that had happened. While they were talking and discussing together, Jesus himself drew near and went with them. But their eyes were kept from recognizing him. *And he said to them, "What is this conversation which you are holding with each other as you walk?"* And they stood still, looking sad. Then one of them, named Cleopas, answered him, "Are you the only visitor to Jerusalem who does not know the things that have happened there in these days?" *And he said to them, "What things?" (Luke 24:13-20)*

Open-ended questions generally begin with words such as when, how, who, and what. Comparing a closed question with an open-ended question will perhaps reinforce the usefulness of acquiring the skill of open-ended communication. Consider the example of a seminarian who, in his formation meeting, states that he wants to lose weight. It is finals week. He adds that he has trouble avoiding desserts when under stress. He also recounts that he saw his physician last week. He was told by his physician that he needed to lose weight because he was a borderline diabetic and already had high blood pressure. A closed question to inquire how the seminarian is doing might be, "Diet going well?" and "Studies going well?" Such a questioning style does not open to a richer and deeper conversation. Consider these open-ended questions: What were you thinking when you received the news from your physician about being pre-diabetic? What effect did that have on you at the time? What do you think you need to do at this time? What else will help? Using open-ended questions, the formator guides the seminarian in cultivating a capacity for deeper self-reflection. Self-reflection is a key for greater self-knowledge. Further, when open-ended questions invite the seminarian to make an appropriate plan of action, personal freedom gradually emerges.

Summarizing

The third communication skill is summarizing. In summarizing, a formator recounts to the seminarian observations made of the seminarian's patterns of thought, feelings and behaviors, be these strengths or weaknesses. These observations are the result of connections the formator made about what the seminarian shared with him or her over the course of formation meetings joined to what he noted in the seminary community. For example, the seminarian says he enjoys being with people. The formator notes, however, that the seminarian does not attend social events at the seminary unless they are obligatory. The formator makes this observation to the seminarian with specific examples. At this point, the seminarian should also be given an opportunity to verify or correct the formator's observations.

The benefits of summarizing are many. It can highlight areas of growth which offer encouragement and hope to the seminarian. Summarizing may serve to point out areas of human formation that need more attention. It can be used to close a formation meeting and plan for a focus of discussion for the next meeting. Summarizing can be used to open the next formation meeting with a view to moving forward with a specific formation goal.

Empathy

I have listed empathy as a skill, but it is an essential quality of accompaniment in likeness to Jesus who walked with the disciples on the way. Empathy in the formator is a quality that embodies the sentiments of the mind and heart of Christ.[49] This disposition communicates respect, understanding, and care for the seminarian.

---

[49] *Ratio,* no. 40, 43, 89; Saint John Eudes *The Life and Kingdom of Jesus in Christian Souls.*

For example, a seminarian is worried about a big philosophy test tomorrow, and he did not do well on his last exam. The formator responds with an empathic voice and body posture: "I hear that you hope you will do better on tomorrow's exam than you did on the last one." This is an example of empathy. There are also several ways to respond that do not exemplify empathy. One is called *reassurance* in which the formator says "You'll do just fine". Another example might be, "I agree, philosophy tests are hard!" That is *Sympathy*. "Did you study?" That is *Judging*. "Let's talk about the Cardinal's game and forget the test." That is *Avoidance*. "There are a lot of tests in life. Don't worry about this one." That is *Minimizing*. "Just study as much as you can and then don't worry about it." That is *Giving Advice*. "When I felt that way as a seminarian, what I did about it was..." That is *Comparing*. "If you think you have it bad, when I was a seminarian we had seminary chores to do in addition to studying." That is *Topping the story. None of those responses exemplify empathy*.[50] In all those cases, an opportunity to display respect, understanding, and care would be lost.

---

[50] Jane Marantz Connor, PhD, Dian Killian, PhD, *Connecting Across Differences*, 2nd edition (Encinitas, California: PuddleDancer Press, 2012), p. 76-78.

Affirmation

Affirmation is a recognition of the seminarian's strivings. Genuine affirmation can incite hope and growth in self-confidence. Another outcome of affirmation can be to keep focused on a goal of formation. For example, "You were resourceful in addressing this situation", "That is a good suggestion", "You are making progress in...", "It's clear you are trying to grow in your..."

Assessment

Accompaniment also includes periodic assessments of the seminarian's level of affective maturity. The *Program for Priestly Formation* states:

> The qualities to be fostered in a human formation program are freedom, openness, honesty and flexibility, joy and inner peace, generosity and justice, personal maturity, interpersonal skills, common sense, aptitude for ministry, and growth "in moral sensibility and character."[51]

Assessing seeks to ascertain the degree to which seminary formation is being interiorized. Is the

---

[51] Committee on Priestly Formation of the United States Conference of Catholic Bishops, *Program of Priestly Formation*, fifth edition. (Washington, D.C.: United States Conference of Catholic Bishops, September, 2006), no. 85.

seminarian exhibiting maturation in his thoughts, feelings and behaviors that embody and manifest a potential for missionary discipleship? Where areas of further growth are needed, practical recommendations are to be made for further human development.

It is a challenge to develop a procedure or means that reflects the level of human maturation of a seminarian and his suitability for ordination. Intellectual formation assessed by grading exams and papers is more objective and quantifiable. Human qualities are not amenable to a "grading" system as such. Human qualities, however, are observable and can be described for assessment.

Markers of human maturation can be articulated in such a manner as to assist formators to assess the presence of these markers in the seminarian.[52] For example, is he patient or impatient with others' shortcomings? Does he have the courage to address concerns in an appropriate manner? Does he express them with love and mercy or is he judgmental? How does he exercise authority? Does he forgive or seek forgiveness? Does he seek to address the needs of others? Does he display missionary zeal to preach and teach the Gospel message by his life? Does he promote an encounter between God and man? Has he ever had a desire for a wife and children? If so, what has he done with this desire? Does he exhibit a readiness to offer his celibate chastity as a sacrifice to be

---

[52] See Chapter Two for more details.

transformed into spiritual fatherhood? How is he a spiritual father for others? This is not a comprehensive list of examples. Evidence of human maturity or lack of maturity can be assessed in the seminarian as he relates to others in the seminary community, as he prays, as he studies, and as he engages in parish ministry assignments.

Summary

Like Jesus who accompanies the disciples on the Road to Emmaus (Luke 24:13-53), the formator accompanies the seminarian on his path of formation. Like Jesus who engages the disciples in conversation on their journey of faith, the formator employs communication skills to guide the seminarian on his journey of faith. Consider the following parallel between Jesus accompanying the disciples and the formator accompanying the seminarian:

Jesus is in their midst. The formator is there, like Christ Himself. Cleopas and the other disciple are on their way to Emmaus. They are emotionally distraught; they do not understand. The seminarian shares his life history with elements of "woe is me". Jesus draws near and travels with them. The formator commits to *accompanying* the seminarian on his journey of formation. Jesus listens to what they say. The formator engages in *reflective listening* seeking to understand what the seminarian is sharing. This encounter builds trust in the relationship. Jesus asks them, "What is this conversation about?" The formator asks *open-ended questions* which opens the door for a deeper and richer conversation. Through this interactive dialogue, Jesus summarizes what has transpired leading the disciples to a new understanding of the happenings of the last days. The formator *summarizes* his observations of the seminarian. These observations are the result of connections made over the course of formation meetings joined to what the formator has noted within the seminary community setting. Summarizing may serve as a means of pointing out areas of human formation that need more attention. The disciples' experience of Jesus is one of being in the Presence of Someone who cares for them and brings them hope. The formator's *empathic responses* engender trust in the seminarian. At their beckoning, Jesus entered the house to stay with them. The formator *affirms* the seminarian's strivings celebrating the seminarian's evolving priestly identity. They recognize Him in the breaking of the bread. The seminarian demonstrates maturation in his thoughts, feelings, and behaviors over the course of seminary formation. The formator *assesses* whether the seminarian manifests a recognizable call to priesthood. Jesus blesses the disciples and departs from them ascending into heaven. They come running back to Jerusalem as missionary disciples. Having been prepared to spread the Gospel as *missionary disciples,* the seminarians are ordained in fulfillment of their vocation to ministerial priesthood.

In closing, the *Ratio* states:

Conversations with formators should be regular and frequent. In this way the seminarian will be able gradually to conform himself to Christ, docile to the action of the Spirit. Such accompaniment must bring together all the aspects of the human person, training him in listening, in dialogue, in the true meaning of obedience and in interior freedom. It is the task of every formator, each according to his proper responsibilities, to assist the seminarian in becoming aware of his condition, of the talents that he has received, and of his frailties, so that he can become ever more receptive to the action of grace.[53]

While the formator engages the seminarian in this formative process, it remains the obligation of the seminarian to cooperate with the Holy Spirit in all aspects of his formation.

The *Program for Priestly Formation*, no. 275 states:

Seminarians are accountable for all aspects of priestly formation within the parameters of the external forum. This includes participation in spiritual exercises, the spiritual direction program, liturgical exercises, and community life as well as the academic and pastoral dimensions of priest-ly formation.

---

[53] *Ratio*, no. 46.

This approach is taken because all the aspects of priestly formation are "intimately interwoven and should not be separated from one another".

Docile to the Holy Spirit, the formator and seminarian bring together all aspects of the human person by engaging in good communication skills.[54]

---

[54] An earlier draft of this paper was presented for the Seminary Formation Council Certificate Program for seminary formators in June, 2017. I am grateful for suggested revisions to this chapter from the following persons: Sister Mary Kathleen Ronan, RSM, PhD, Sister Mary Prudence Allen, RSM, PhD, Sister Mary Cora Uryase, RSM, PhD and Rev. Msgr. Thomas Caserta, DMin.

CHAPTER FOUR

Formators' Assessment Templates

Sketch by Heinrich Hofmann (1893)

**Forming Seminary Formators
in the Art of Accompaniment**

The details of the fundamental principles underlying each template are referenced in a footnote with corresponding chapter pages. The first template proposes steps for dialogue and instruction directed toward establishing a relationship of accompaniment between the seminarian and the formator. The second template offers questions to assist the formator in assessing a seminarian's level of affective maturity. The third template offers the formator instruction on how to enter into an effective dialogue of listening, understanding, encouraging, and challenging the seminarian. The fourth template is an exercise for four or more formators. They are invited to enter into a formative dialogue with their peers and subsequently discuss how the principles of accompaniment were employed.

The Road to Accompaniment[55]

STEP 1:   Obtain Background Information from Seminarian's Seminary Application and in Dialogue with the Seminarian as Groundwork for Accompaniment

STEP 2:   Clarify with the Seminarian Expectations of Accompaniment

STEP 3:   Describe to the Seminarian the Process of Discovering God's

---

[55] Cf. pp. 12-32. The template may also be downloaded as a PDF from En Route Books and Media http://enroutebooksandmedia.com/artofaccompaniment/

Design through Accompaniment in his "Review of Life"

STEP 4: What are Areas in Which Affective Growth and Development Can Be Fostered in Accompanying this Seminarian

STEP 5: Calling the Seminarian to Take On the Sentiments of Christ

Markers of Human Maturation in Seminary Formation: Becoming a Gift for Others[56]

There are six interrelated markers of human maturation significant to the formation of seminarians:

self-knowledge,
self-direction,
self-control,
self-discipline,
self-governance, and
spiritual fatherhood.[57]

---

[56] Cf. pp. 33-56. The template may also be downloaded as a PDF from En Route Books and Media http://enroutebooksandmedia.com/artofaccompaniment/

[57] These markers were first described and presented in the chapter "Significant Markers of Human Maturation Applied to the Selection and Formation of Seminarians" (Sister Marysia Weber, *Seminary Journal*,

They are listed in ascending order of affective maturity.

Self-Awareness to Self-Knowledge

Questions to assess whether a seminarian is exhibiting this maturational marker:

☐ Does he exhibit:

- The ability to acknowledge his feelings?

- Emotional stability?

- A desire to gain a more complete and accurate knowledge of his motivations?

- Appropriate self-disclosure?

☐ Does he manifest a willingness to admit to mistakes?

☐ Is he appropriately self-reliant with a capacity to trust himself yet, at the same time, able to rely on and entrust himself to others?

15(1): 35-41 (2009). The specific names of the markers have evolved and changes will be noted.

Questions to assess whether a seminarian exhibits limited self-knowledge:

☐ Are the seminarian's relationships needy and emotionally-charged?

☐ Do his relationships terminate in frustration because of his neediness or emotional outbursts?

☐ Does he withdraw when emotionally conflicted?

☐ Does he exhibit excessively ingratiating behaviors?

☐ Does he give evidence of feeling undervalued?

☐ Does he give evidence of being self-focused? For example:

- Is he mostly about me, my, and mine?
- Is he unaware of what is going on around him?

☐ Does he frequently avoid acknowledging personal faults?

☐ Does he prefer to have others make decisions for him so as to avoid responsibility?

Self-Direction

Questions to assess whether a seminarian exhibits appropriate self-direction:

☐ Is he able to receive criticism with docility and address it?

☐ Does he exhibit appropriate initiative?

☐ Can he accept a difficult situation and function within it?

☐ Has he achieved the capacity to differ with others' opinions without dismissing those with whom he disagrees?

☐ Is he comfortable in the presence of authority persons without antagonism or withdrawal from relationship?

Questions to assess whether a seminarian exhibits limited self-direction:

☐ Does he prefer to have others make decisions for him?

☐ Does he demonstrate excessive compliance?

☐ Is he rigid and lacking a capacity for flexibility in interactions?

☐ Does he seek the attention of authority persons to build up his self-worth?

☐ Does he use others for what they can do for him?

☐ Does he exhibit a lack of personal autonomy and initiative?

☐ Does he exhibit ambivalence and self-doubt?

☐ Does he lack a capacity to cooperate with others?

☐ Is he frequently in conflict with authority persons?

Self-Control

Questions to assess whether a seminarian exhibits self-control:

☐ Does the seminarian exercise responsible

stewardship in his use of time and resources?

☐ Does he exhibit a healthy sense of pride and self-competence from his work?

☐ Is he able to delay gratification for a future or greater good?

☐ Does he have a capacity for balancing harmony and diversity?

☐ Does he experience a heightened sense of fulfillment through collaboration with others in ministry?

☐ Does he encourage those with whom he is working to search for the good in others' ideas?

Questions to assess whether a seminarian exhibits limited self-control:

☐ Does he exhibit strong emotional reactions when someone "crosses" him?

☐ Does he feel incompetent or undervalued?

☐ Is he excessively critical of others or himself?

☐ Does he lack a sense of joy in authentic self-giving?

☐ Is he bothered by feelings of inferiority and inadequacy?

☐ Does he exhibit frequent negative murmuring or sarcasm?

☐ Does he exhibit apathy or "burnout" when his work performance does not compensate for his low self-esteem?

☐ Does he lack the capacity for appropriate delayed gratification?

Self-Discipline

Questions to assess whether a seminarian exhibits self-discipline:

☐ Does he exhibit appropriate interpersonal boundaries?

☐ Does he relate respectfully to women and men?

☐ Does he exercise discretion in his use of technology and choices of entertainment?

☐ Does he make choices that enable him to refrain from addictive behaviors? (For example, regarding his use of alcohol and use of the Internet)

☐ Does he demonstrate realistic problem solving skills?

Questions to assess whether a seminarian exhibits limited self-discipline:

☐ Does he have enmeshed relationships with poor interpersonal boundaries?

☐ Does he have more acquaintances than friendships?

☐ Does the seminarian rely heavily on the role he plays to define his sense of personal adequacy and security?

☐ Does he have to "prove" his adequacy by his performance?

☐ Does he engage in pleasurable excesses?

Self-Governance

Questions to assess whether a seminarian exhibits self-governance:

☐ Does he demonstrate sound prudential judgment in his choices?

☐ Is he able to form relationships that are responsible, respectful, and marked by integrity?

☐ Does he manifest an ability to forgive others and seek forgiveness for personal short-comings?

☐ Does he understand suffering in his own life and respond accordingly?

☐ Does he show compassion to those who are suffering?

☐ Does he exhibit faithful perseverance in fulfilling commitments?

☐ Is he faithful to the vocation to which he is identifying?

☐ Does he address self-denial, loneliness, and celibacy in a mature manner that also serve to enrich his life?

Questions to assess whether a seminarian exhibits limited self-governance:

☐ Does he function poorly in a stressful or delicate situation?

☐ Does he fail to fulfill commitments he has made?

☐ Are his interpersonal relationships characterized by superficiality?

☐ Does he demonstrate a limited sensitivity to the sufferings of others?

☐ Is he ambivalent about his sexual orientation, moral values, or commitments?

☐ Is celibacy a burden for him?

☐ Does he lack a capacity for fidelity to the teachings of the Catholic Church?

Spiritual Fatherhood

Questions to assess a seminarian's disposition for spiritual fatherhood:

☐ Does he manifest a "strong, lively, personal love" of Jesus Christ?

☐ Does he exhibit the capacity to mentor?

☐ Is he an instrument directing others to God?

☐ Does he exhibit a disposition for service?

☐ Is he enriched by his service?

☐ Is he striving for conversion from attitudes contrary to pastoral charity?

☐ Does he consistently exhibit a capacity for self-sacrifice trusting in God?

☐ Does he display the capacity to renounce the goods of marriage for spiritual fatherhood?

Questions to assess a seminarian who has a limited disposition for spiritual fatherhood:

☐ Does his love for himself surpass his love for

others?

☐ Does he prefer "privileged" work?

☐ Does he manifest a need to be "successful" in ministry?

☐ Does he use relationships with others for self-aggrandizement?

☐ Does he manifest inappropriate possessiveness of his gifts?

☐ Is he insensitive to what is going on around him?

☐ Does he lack a capacity to be self-sacrificing and altruistic?

Narrative Assessment[58]

Seminarian:

Year in Formation:

Formator:

Date:

- What are the seminarian's strengths presently in his formation process? Give specific examples as reflected in significant markers of human maturation:

- Where does he have room to grow? Give specific examples as reflected in significant markers of human maturation:

- List practical recommendations to address vocational growth and development:

---

[58] The template may also be downloaded as a PDF from En Route Books and Media http://enroutebooksandmedia.com/artofaccompanimen t/

Communication Skills for Formative Dialogue Directed Toward Missionary Discipleship[59]

Effective formative dialogue requires six skills:

1. reflective (or active) listening, 2. open-ended questions, 3. summarizing responses, 4. empathy, 5. affirmation, and 6. assessment.

1. Reflective Listening: A strategy of communication involving two steps:

1. Formator seeks to understand what the seminarian meant by what he said.
2. Formator seeks to confirm the accuracy of what he understood.

A common obstacle is that the formator assumes he or she knows what the seminarian means. For example, he or she hears the seminarian say, "I wish I was more outgoing." The seminarian may be thinking:

- "I feel lonely and I want to have more friends."
- "I get very nervous when I have to speak to a

---

[59] Cf. pp. 57-72. The template may also be downloaded as a PDF from En Route Books and Media http://enroutebooksandmedia.com/artofaccompanimen t/

group of people."
- "I should spend more time getting to know people."
- "I can't think of anything to say when I am with people."

In addition to the words chosen by the seminarian, attention should be paid to the seminarian's non-verbal communication. 93% of communication occurs non-verbally (as shown earlier):

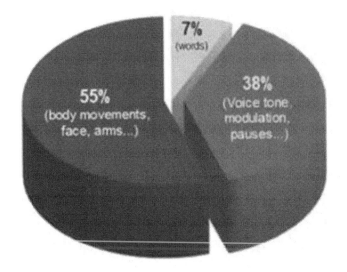

For example, tone of voice can convey two very different meanings to identical words. ("You were feeling uncomfortable?" or "You were feeling uncomfortable.")

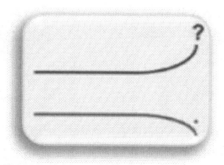

2. Open-Ended Questions

Posing open-ended questions offers an invitation to describe an experience in greater detail. For example:

- What was it like to hear/learn...?
- What were you thinking at the time?
- What have you thought about since?
- What effect did that have on you?
- What effect does this have on you now?
- What do you think you need to do at this time?
- What else will help?

Open-ended questions facilitate deeper self-reflection.

3. Summarizing Responses

The formator recounts observations made of the patterns of thought, feelings, and behaviors of the seminarian. The seminarian should also be given an opportunity to verify or correct the observations of the formator.

4. Empathy

Empathy engenders a sense of being cared about, respected and understood. A seminarian is worried about a big philosophy test tomorrow, and he did not do well on his last exam. The formator responds: "You hope you will do better on tomorrow's exam than you did on the last one." This is an example of **empathy.**

There are several ways to respond that do not exemplify empathy[60]:

- "You'll do just fine." – **Reassurance**
- "I agree, philosophy tests are hard!" – **Sympathy**
- "Let's talk about the Cardinal's game and forget the test." – **Avoidance**
- "There are a lot of tests in life. Don't worry about this one." – **Minimizing**
- "Just study as much as you can and then don't worry about it." – **Giving Advice**
- "When I felt that way as a seminarian, what I did about it was..." – **Comparing**

---

[60] Adapted from J.M. Connor and D. Killian, 2012 PuddleDancer Press

- "If you think you have it bad, we had seminary chores to do when I was a seminarian in addition to studying." – **Topping the Story**

5. Affirmation

Affirmation is a recognition of the seminarian's strivings. It incites hope and growth in self-confidence. By providing affirmation, the formator helps the seminarian remain focused on a formation goal. For example:

- "You were resourceful in addressing this situation."
- "That is a good suggestion."
- "You are making progress in..."
- "It's clear you are trying to grow in your..."

6. Assessment

Accompaniment also includes periodic assessments of the seminarian's level of affective maturity. Assessing seeks to ascertain the degree to which seminary formation has been interiorized. For example:

- Has the seminarian exhibited maturation in his thoughts, feelings and behaviors that embody and manifest a potential for missionary discipleship?
- Where areas of further growth are needed,

practical recommendations are to be made for furthering human development.

- Details of associated markers of human maturation and associated questions are in chapter two.

While the formator engages the seminarian in this formative process, it remains the obligation of the seminarian to cooperate with the Holy Spirit in all aspects of his formation.

Formators' Practicum Exercise: The Art of the Question in the Service of Accompaniment

Purpose:

To seek a deeper understanding of the seminarian's experience in order to accompany him.

This exercise, utilizing four formators, is intended to assist formators in developing the communication skills described in Chapter 3 and outlined in the communication skills template.[61]

The Art of the Question

Reject the thought that you already know what the seminarian will say.

Questions should be:

• Open-ended to draw conversation (not ques-

_____

[61] Cf. pp. 87-92

tions that can be answered simply with a yes or no)

- Thought provoking – for depth

Practicals

Four persons to play the roles of formator, seminarian and two participant-observers (equipped with pen and paper).

Arrange seating as shown in the diagram

Appoint a timekeeper (the entire exercise is 40 minutes, with four 10-minute segments)

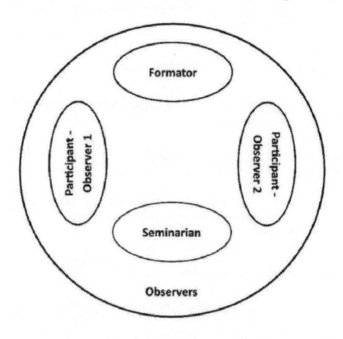

The participant-observers write down the actual words said by the formator and seminarian.

Segment 1 (10 minutes) – Dialogue between formator and seminarian

Formator begins with the following suggested questions:

How did you come to know a vocation to the priesthood? What do you hope for? What are your greatest concerns?

Describe an experience of when you felt grateful? Sorrowful? Hopeful? Joyful? Peaceful?

In any of the above experiences:

What effect did this situation have on you? On others?

How did you respond?

If you could, would you do anything differently? How would you make it happen?

Segment 2 (10 minutes) – Conversation between participant-observers

Discuss the actual words and nonverbals the formator and seminarian used.

Propose questions, if any, the formator might ask of the seminarian for deeper reflection in Segment 3.

Segment 3 (10 minutes) – Dialogue between formator and seminarian about participant-observers' conversation

What stirred in you, the formator, as you listened to what the participant-observers said about your dialogue with the seminarian? Did you hear something that surprised you?

Does this prompt you to consider modifying how you ask questions?

Can you think of a way to elicit a greater depth of response from the seminarian?

As seminarian, is there anything you would have liked the formator to ask you?

Segment 4 (10 minutes) – Group reflection on the formator's engagement of the seminarian

What questions, if any, did the formator ask the seminarian that facilitated his coming to a deeper self-awareness?

What other questions might the formator have

asked the seminarian to facilitate a deeper self-awareness?

What nonverbals did the formator use to reinforce his accompaniment of the seminarian?

(Adapted from www.iirp.edu and Rundell, F 2003)

Appendix

The following appendix by Sister Joseph Marie Ruessmann, RSM, is a comprehensive study of the historical development of the concept of internal and external fora. Her conclusion offers elements to be included in a statement of policy concerning confidentiality and inserted into seminary handbooks.

Confidentiality and Knowledge Requirements in Seminary Formation

by

Sister Joseph Marie Ruessmann, RSM,
JD, JCD, MBA

This article approaches the topic of confidentiality in seminary formation by applying the principles presented in the Church documents on priestly formation since those documents, besides the Code of Canon Law, are what would be considered the norms for seminaries to follow. The hierarchy of authority behind the documents is:

1) *The Code of Canon Law* (1983)

2) Documents of the Apostolic See

    a) Documents issued by the Congregation for Clergy (in January 2013, it became responsible for formation in seminaries), primarily:

        Ratio Fundamentalis Institutionis Sacerdotalis (issued on Dec.8, 2016) ("*Ratio*").

    b) Documents issued by the Congregation for Catholic Education before 2013, primarily:

        1. "Guidelines for the Use of Psychology in the Admission and Formation of Candidates for the Priesthood" (2008);

        2. Final Report on Apostolic Visitation of Seminaries in the United States (Dec.15, 2008);

        3. "Instruction Concerning the Criteria for the Discernment of Vocations with regard to Persons with Homosexual Tendencies in view of their Admission to the Seminary and to Holy Orders" (2005);

4. "Instruction to the Episcopal Conferences on the Admission to Seminary of Candidates Coming from Other Seminaries or Religious Families" (1996);

5. "Directives Concerning the Preparation of Seminary Educators" (1993) [*Origins* 23:22 (Jan. 27, 1994) 557-571; also published as "Directives on the Preparation of Formators in Seminaries," in *Enchiridion Vaticanum* 13 (1996) 3224-3253.

c) Documents issued by the Congregation for Divine Worship and the Discipline of the Sacraments, primarily:

"Circular Letter to the Most Reverend Diocesan Bishops and other Ordinaries with Canonical Faculties to Admit to Sacred Orders concerning: Scrutinies regarding the Suitability of Candidates for Orders" (1997).

d) [for members of religious institutes] Documents issued by the Congregation for Institutes of Consecrated Life and Societies of Apostolic Life, primarily:

Directives on Formation in Religious Institutes (1990).

3) United States Conference of Catholic Bishops, *Program for Priestly Formation*, 5th ed. (2005)(approved originally by the Congregation for Catholic Education, and approved in 2015 for another five years by the Congregation for Clergy)("*PPF*").

The *Ratio* promulgated by the Congregation for Clergy in December 2016 is similar to the previous *Ratio* (which was promulgated in 1985 by the Congregation for Catholic Education) in that it includes guidelines and norms regarding vocation promotion, minor and major seminaries, the four pillars of formation, the stages of formation, and roles of persons at the seminary; and calls for the conferences of bishops of the nations to submit their own *Ratio Nationalis* to the Congregation in conformity with the Congregation's *Ratio*. The new *Ratio* has a different tone than the previous *Ratio*. It emphasizes integrated and communitarian formation, the unity of formation, and personal accompaniment and community accompaniment of the seminarian, in an atmosphere of mutual trust.[62] The seminarian is to be formed to interior maturity and interior freedom, not just "demonstrating a 'veneer of virtuous habits,' a merely external and formalistic obedience to abstract principles."[63] The seminarian is to let himself be known, relating to

---

[62] See nos. 3, 44-53, 90, 92.
[63] no. 41.

his formators with transparency; and have frequent and regular conversations with his formators.[64]

The old *Ratio* spoke of "superiors."[65] The new *Ratio* instead speaks of "formators," which include at least the rector and the spiritual director,[66] and, depending on the size of the seminary, could include others, such as a coordinator of human formation.[67] The *Ratio* sometimes lists "formators" separately from "spiritual directors," applying the text to both groups equally.[68]

In this article, the term "formator" is used to mean only those whom are called "formation advisors/mentors and directors" in the *PPF*,[69] to distinguish this person from the spiritual director. (The *Ratio* includes both persons in its use of the term "formators," except where it refers separately to the spiritual director.)

Part A. Confidentiality requirements regarding the inner life of seminarians

Two canons of the Code of Canon Law are the bases of confidentiality requirements in seminary formation: c. 220 regarding the right (of everyone) to a

---

[64] nos. 45, 46.

[65] nos. 27-31.

[66] These two persons are the minimum formators required by the Code of Canon Law for a seminary. See *Ratio*, no. 133.

[67] no. 137.

[68] See section C4d2C below.

[69] no. 80.

good reputation and to protect one's privacy, and c. 240 §2 regarding the prohibition against asking a seminarian's spiritual director for his opinion as to whether the seminarian should be ordained.

1) Right to a good reputation and to protection of privacy

The seminarian has the right to his good reputation and to protect his privacy. Canon 220 states, "No one is permitted to harm illegitimately the good reputation which a person possesses nor to injure the right of any person to protect his or her own privacy."

One of the sources of canon 220 was the Second Vatican Council's pastoral constitution on the Church, *Gaudium et Spes*. *Gaudium et Spes* includes the rights to a good reputation and to protection of one's privacy as basic human rights, which originate in the natural law.[70] The document describes the forum of conscience as "man's most secret core, and his sanctuary, [where] he is alone with God whose voice echoes in his depths."[71]

The right to protect one's privacy is the right not to have to manifest one's conscience, with "conscience" understood as one's psychological or moral intimacy; the intimacy of one's interior.[72] Canon

---

[70] no. 26.

[71] no. 16.

[72] See Secretariat of State, *Instruction*, 6 Aug. 1976, issued to the pontifical representatives throughout the world to share with the bishops' conferences of their

220 is based on the dignity of the person, his right to guard his interior life, as a part of his person, from invasion or intrusion, as he might guard his property.[73]

According to an Instruction issued by the Vatican Secretary of State in 1976, the standard for the protection of a person's right to protect his privacy under c. 220 is that his consent be previous, explicit, informed, and free.[74] The Congregation for

---

countries; and referred to in a 1998 decision of the Congregation for Clergy; as reported in Rev. Gregory Ingels, "Protecting the Right to Privacy when examining issues affecting the life and ministry of clerics and religious," in *Studia canonica* 34 (2000), pp. 439-466, p. 444.

Some canonists would interpret the canonical right to "privacy" more broadly. In his commentary on Code c.220, Fr. Daniel Cenalmor states, "...the right to one's own privacy also extends, within the Church, to everything that does not fall under the scope of the public nor commonly known..." *Exegetical Commentary on the Code of Canon Law*, University of Navarre (Midwest Theological Forum, Chicago, 2004), vol. II/1, pp. 126-132, p. 131.

[73] See Marcozzi, Vittorio, SJ, "Il diritto all propria intimità nel nuovo codice di diritto canonico," in La Civiltà Cattolica, Anno 134 (1983), vol. IV, pp. 573-580.

[74] The Instruction, which was issued to the pontifical representatives throughout the world, stated, "*It is illegal for anyone, even religious or diocesan superiors, to enter into the psychological or moral intimacy of a person without having obtained his previous, explicit, informed, and absolutely free consent...*"

Clergy confirmed the requirement of consent in a case of hierarchical recourse to the Congregation in 1998, agreeing with a priest that his bishop could not oblige him to undergo a psychological evaluation. The Congregation stated, "It is the consistent teaching of the Magisterium that investigation of the intimate psychological and moral status of the interior life of any member of the Christian faithful cannot be carried on except with the consent of the one to undergo such evaluation..."[75]

The "previous, explicit, informed, and free" requirement for consent seems to apply to psychological investigations (assessments, evaluations, consultations, and therapy), which have as their intent the probing of a person's interior life. The psychologist attempts to enter the person's "inner core," having him reveal his psyche, inducing disclosure, by various means, such as personality tests. This might be done, for example, on behalf of a seminary that is trying to determine if a person is suitable for entrance into the seminary.

It seems that the consent requirement does not apply to seminary spiritual directors and formators

---

See my article "Internal Forum and External Forum in the Seminary Revisited—Part 2: The Role of the Rector and Formators," in *Seminary Journal*, Fall 2012, vol. 18, no. 2, pp. 95-102, pp. 95-96. See also Rev. Gregory Ingels, "Protecting the Right to Privacy...", pp. 443-444.

[75] See Ingels, "Protecting the Right to Privacy...", p.445.

(or the Bishop or rectors) in their questioning of seminarians[76] because:

1. The Vatican Instruction and the Congregation for Clergy's decision, in presenting the consent requirement, spoke of it only in regard to obliging someone to undergo psychological testing or a psychological evaluation. They did not talk about the direct questioning of a subject by a superior.[77]

2. In the Church documents on priestly

---

[76] Nonetheless, since the seminarian's expectations might differ from those of the seminary, it seems advisable for the seminary to obtain from each new seminarian a signed agreement in regard to the seminary's policies. See below, the Conclusion.

[77] The Instruction to the pontifical representatives was accompanied by an article in 1976 by Vittorio Marcozzi, SJ, about the right to privacy: "Indagini psicologiche e diritti della persona," in La Civiltà Cattolica, Anno 127 (1976), vol. II, pp. 541-551. The article was about the violation of a person's right to privacy by obliging him to undergo psychological testing or evaluation, not about direct questioning by a superior.

In his commentary on Code c.220, Fr. Daniel Cenalmor states, "...no one can force another to let one's personal privacy be analyzed; one must first have explicit, informed and absolutely free permission." He cites Fr. Marcozzi's second article (see n. 12 above). *Exegetical Commentary on the Code of Canon Law*, University of Navarre (Midwest Theological Forum, Chicago, 2004), vol. II/1, pp. 126-132, p. 131.

formation since the Second Vatican Council, all of the references to the candidate's right to privacy relate to asking him to undergo psychological testing or evaluation, or to the results of psychological testing and other confidential materials.[78] None of the passages on privacy refer to questioning of seminarians by seminary staff persons or to seminarians' conversations with them.

3. The consent requirement does not seem practicable for conversations or dialogue with someone with whom one has an ongoing relationship, regular interaction, and with whom one lives in community; and

4. The consent requirement does not fit with the roles of the spiritual director and formator, who are to have frequent (regular) meetings with the seminarian for in-depth conversations.[79]

Even if c. 220 would not prevent seminary spiritual directors or formators (or Bishop or

---

[78] See *The Gift of the Priestly Vocation: Ratio Fundamentalis Institutionis Sacerdotalis* ("*Ratio*"), L'Osservatore Romano, Vatican City 12/08/16, no. 194; "Apostolorum Successores," Directory for the Pastoral Ministry of Bishops, Feb. 22, 2004, no. 88; *Guidelines for the Use of Psychology in the Admission and Formation of Candidates for the Priesthood*, June 28, 2008, nos. 12, 13; USCCB's Program for Priestly Formation, 5th ed. (2005) ("*PPF*"), nos. 52, 57.

[79] See C4d below.

rector) from asking a seminarian about his interior life ("inner core"), they may not require or insist upon a self-revelation. This can be deduced from the fact that seminary spiritual directors and formators may not oblige a seminarian to have a psychological consultation. The spiritual director can "suggest to the candidate that he undergo a psychological consultation – without, however, ever demanding it."[80] "If the candidate, faced with a motivated request by the formators, should refuse to undergo a psychological consultation, the formators will not force his will in any way. Instead, they will prudently proceed in the work of discernment with the knowledge they already have..."[81]

Requiring someone to undergo a psychological consultation would be to oblige someone indirectly to make a revelation of his "inner core." The fact that a spiritual director or formator cannot force a revelation of a seminarian's inner core through another implies that the spiritual director or formator cannot force it himself directly. He can ask for a self-revelation (a manifestation of "conscience") by a seminarian, but cannot insist on it. The c. 220 right to privacy would allow a seminarian to refuse to discuss personal matters.[82]

---

[80] Congregation for Catholic Education, *Guidelines for the Use of Psychology...*, no.14.

[81] *Guidelines*, no. 12.

[82] His refusal to answer, though, could have consequences. The spiritual director would have the option to stop being his spiritual director, and the

Code c. 246 §4 recognizes this when it says that each seminarian should have a spiritual director to whom he "can confidently open his conscience." The use of the word "can" instead of "ought to" or "must" indicates that the opening of one's conscience cannot be forced.

Similarly, the Code of Canon Law, in c. 630 §5 (which would apply to seminarians in religious institutes), forbids religious superiors from inducing a religious to make a manifestation of his conscience. This means that a religious superior may not insist on a manifestation, or put pressure on a member to make a manifestation. If a superior asks a member for a self-revelation and the member refuses, the superior must accept his refusal.[83]

2) Spiritual direction as a confidential relationship, "in the internal forum"

The USCCB's *Program for Priestly Formation* ("*PPF*") states, "Seminarians should confide their personal history, personal relationships, prayer experiences, the cultivation of virtues, their temptations, and other significant topics to their

---

seminary could tell the seminarian that he may not continue at the seminary if he does not cooperate.

[83] See my article "Internal Forum and External Forum in the Seminary Revisited—Part 2: The Role of the Rector and Formators," in *Seminary Journal*, Fall 2012, vol. 18, no. 2, pp. 95-102, p. 97.

spiritual director...."[84] Spiritual direction is a confidential relationship, subject to the rules of moral theology regarding the extent of obligation of secrecy for the matter divulged.[85]

In the Code of Canon Law, the term "internal forum" signifies the exercise of the power of jurisdiction in the Church in a hidden way.[86] The Code does not use the term "internal forum" in relation to spiritual direction since the spiritual director does not exercise the power of jurisdiction. The Code does not say that the spiritual director is in the internal forum or that the spiritual director of a seminarian may never reveal to anyone that which he learned in spiritual direction. It only says that the opinion of the confessor and of the spiritual director may not be asked in regard to whether to admit a seminarian to Orders or to dismiss him from the seminary.[87]

The Congregation for Clergy, in its document on spiritual direction, does not say that the spiritual director, even in the seminary, is in the internal forum. It says only that the "exercise of the power of jurisdiction in the Church should always respect the reserve and the silence of the spiritual

---

[84] Fifth edition, no. 128.

[85] See my article "Internal Forum and External Forum in the Seminary Revisited—Part 1: The Role of the Spiritual Director," in *Seminary Journal,* Fall 2012, vol. 18, no. 2, pp. 89-94, p. 91.

[86] See "Internal Forum and External Forum in the Seminary Revisited—Part 1, p. 89.

[87] c. 240 §2.

director."[88] In its *Ratio*, the Congregation for Clergy states that the spiritual director is in the internal forum: the spiritual director has the "responsibility for the spiritual journey of the seminarians in the internal forum."[89]

The Congregation for Catholic Education, in its report on its visitation of seminaries in the United States, says, "There is confusion, in places, as to what the internal forum is (it covers only sacramental confession and spiritual direction..."[90] In another document, the Congregation says that the spiritual director, although he is bound to secrecy, represents the Church in the internal forum.[91]

The Congregation for Institutes of Consecrated Life and Societies of Apostolic Life ("CIVCSVA") [for members of religious institutes] also talks of the spiritual director being in the internal forum: "...religious should have a person available to them, who may be called a spiritual director or spiritual counselor, for the internal, even non-sacramental,

---

[88] *The Priest, Minister of Divine Mercy: An Aid for Confessors and Spiritual Directors* (Libreria Editrice Vaticana, 2011), no. 103.

[89] *Ratio*, no. 136.

[90] *Final Report on Apostolic Visitation of Seminaries in the United States*, Dec. 15, 2008, p. 14, no. 6.

[91] *Instruction concerning the Criteria for the Discernment of Vocations with regard to Persons with Homosexual Tendencies in view of their Admission to the Seminary and to Holy Orders*, Aug. 31, 2005, no. 3.

forum."[92]

The *PPF* mentions four times that the spiritual director is in the internal forum.[93] For example, it states, "Disclosures that a seminarian makes in the course of spiritual direction belong to the internal forum. Consequently, the spiritual director is held to the strictest confidentiality concerning information received in spiritual direction. He may neither reveal it nor use it."[94] It also states, "Since spiritual direction takes place in the internal forum, the relationship of seminarians to their spiritual director is a privileged and confidential one. Spiritual directors may not participate in the evaluation of those they currently direct or whom they directed in the past."[95]

Part B. Requirements for knowledge about the seminarian

The above principles of confidentiality restrict access to information about seminarians. On the other hand, Church documents indicate the need for limits on confidentiality in seminary formation for more fruitful formation of the candidates, for the sake of ordaining only suitable candidates, and

---

[92] *Directives on Formation in Religious Institutes*, Feb. 2, 1990, no. 63.

[93] Nos. 80, 134, 332, 333

[94] no. 134.

[95] no. 133.

for the early detection of problems in candidates. [96]

1) Openness as docility for formation

The seminarian needs to be open with his formators and spiritual director in order to be formed and directed spiritually to be suitable as a priest. Seminarians should be open and trusting not only with the spiritual director, but also with the formators. Trust and openness by the seminarian shows a mature appreciation of authority, and shows docility and obedience; an acceptance of God's will as manifested through one's superiors; and the desire for self-knowledge as a means to open oneself to conversion.[97]

2) Knowledge for determining suitability

The Code of Canon Law requires that the Bishop ensure that the candidate has the necessary qualities:

> "Only those are to be promoted to orders who, in the prudent judgment of their own bishop... all things considered, have integral faith, are

---

[96] Federal and state laws protecting minors are a further reason for limits on confidentiality in the seminary. The viewing of child pornography, such as on the Internet, is a crime in many states. Also, statutes in many states require anyone who has information about the sexual abuse of a child to report it to the state.

[97] See section C3 below.

moved by the right intention, have the requisite knowledge, possess a good reputation, and are endowed with integral morals and proven virtues and the other physical and psychic qualities in keeping with the order to be received." [98]

The Code requires that the suitability of the seminarian for ordination be positively proven:

"For a bishop conferring ordination by his own right to proceed to the ordination, he must be sure...that, after the investigation has been conducted according to the norm of law, positive arguments have proven the suitability of the candidate." [99]

The Congregation for Clergy, in the *Ratio*, has elaborated that this suitability must be clearly demonstrated and reasons given or, in other words *"positive arguments give moral certainty of the suitability of the candidate,"* and not simply the absence of problematic situations...." [100]

The seminarian's rights to privacy and to protect his reputation are limited by the common good of the Church. Ecclesiastical authority is entitled to regulate, in view of the common good, the exercise of rights that are proper to Christ's

---

[98] c. 1029.

[99] c. 1052 §1.

[100] *Ratio* no. 206. See also *Guidelines for the Use of Psychology...*, no. 11.

faithful.[101] The ordaining of only suitable ministers is part of the common good of the Church. The suitability of a priest affects everyone—himself, his bishop, his fellow priests, the faithful he serves, and the public who see him as a representative of the Church. The priest is a public figure and should be a model, not a source of damage or scandal.

3) Timely detection of problems

The common good of the Church requires timely detection of problems in candidates to the priesthood. Detecting and addressing defects in candidates as early as possible is a way to help them and to avoid problems later. The Congregation for Catholic Education has stated, "The timely discernment of possible problems that block the vocational journey can only be of great benefit for the person, for the vocational institutions and for the Church"; and "...errors in discerning vocations are not rare, and in all too many cases, psychological defects, sometimes of a pathological kind, reveal themselves only after ordination to the priesthood. Detecting defects earlier would help avoid many tragic experiences."[102]

The Congregation for Divine Worship and the Discipline of the Sacraments, in 1997, wrote:

---

[101] c. 223 §2.

[102] *Guidelines for the Use of Psychology...*, no. 8, no. 4, respectively.

In the course of its examination and processing of the procedural acts relating to the dispensation from the obligations of the clerical state together with dismissal from the same state. It is often clear that among the reasons for the numerous defections of both priests and deacons is a certain haste in the analysis of the suitability of their promotion to Sacred Orders.

In these cases there have been departures from the requirement of ensuring, prior to Ordination, the absence of defects, impediments and irregularities in the candidate and the presence of the positive requirements dictated by prudence and prescribed by canonical norms, and an omission, too, of a serious evaluation of certain symptoms of un-suitability that have come to light during the years of formation.[103]

The *PPF* also recommends apprising seminarians of their progress and prospects as early as possible:

> • "Each seminary must provide a procedure for the evaluation of the seminarians. As part of this procedure, each seminary should ensure...that the seminarians are apprised of their progress as early as possible in their formation, particularly if

---

[103] Cover Letter Nov. 28, 1997, to the Circular Letter, "Scrutinies regarding the Suitability of Candidates for Orders," Prot. 589/97, Nov. 10, 1997.

there are concerns..."[104]

- "Seminarians who lack the positive qualities for continuing in formation should not be advanced in the seminary program. They should be advised to leave the seminary. Seminarians not recommended for advancement should be notified as early as possible and in a constructive manner...."[105]

Part C. Resolution of potential tensions

Part A spoke of norms pertaining to restrictions on obtaining or revealing a revelation of a seminarian's interior life. Part B spoke of the need for openness by seminarians and the Church's need for in-depth knowledge of candidates for the priesthood.

This Part C will present the norms that represent how the Church has resolved the potential tension or conflict between the two aspects. The resolution is by Church norms that:

1. provide, in unusual cases, for action by the spiritual director;
2. provide, on a periodic basis, for information on a candidate through evaluations done by his fellow seminarians; and
3. (primarily) require self-revelation by the

---

[104] no. 274.
[105] no. 287.

seminarian to his formators, including through a psychologist.

1) Actions of the spiritual director

The spiritual director is to act in regard to (important) problems of which he learns in spiritual direction.

1a) Refer seminarian to formator or a psychologist

If a seminarian indicates to his spiritual director personal problems that would affect his suitability as a priest, the spiritual director needs to act so that the issues be resolved. He should tell the seminarian to tell the formator about the problem, and/or refer the seminarian to a psychologist. As the *PPF* says, "Care should be taken to ensure that issues of human formation that properly belong to the external forum are not limited to the spiritual direction relationship for their resolution."[106]

According to the Congregation for Catholic Education, the spiritual director sometimes should ask the seminarian to have a psychological consultation:

> ...the spiritual director can find that, in order to clear up any doubts that are otherwise irresolvable and to proceed with greater

---

[106] no. 131.

certainty in the discernment and in spiritual accompaniment, he needs to suggest to the candidate that he undergo a psychological consultation–without, however, ever demanding it.

Should the spiritual director request that the candidate undergo a psychological consultation, it is desirable that the candidate, as well as informing the spiritual director himself about the results of the consultation, will likewise inform the external-forum formator, especially if the spiritual director himself will have invited him to do this.[107]

1b) Dissuade an unsuitable seminarian

If the seminarian is unsuitable, the spiritual director should dissuade him from proceeding towards ordination.

The Congregation for Catholic Education has spoken of the spiritual director's duty to dissuade an unsuitable candidate:

In the discernment concerning the suitability for ordination, the spiritual director has an important task. Although he is bound to secrecy, he represents the Church in the internal forum....If a candidate practises homosexuality or presents deep-seated homosexual tendencies, his spiritual director as well as his

---

[107] *Guidelines for the Use of Psychology*..., no. 14.

confessor have the duty to dissuade him in conscience from proceeding towards ordination.[108]

The *PPF* speaks of the spiritual director's role of assessing the progress of the candidate against certain criteria, which implies the need for the spiritual director to act if the criteria are not met:

> ...the spiritual direction process must take into account the limited time of the program and preparation for ordination and that, therefore, one ought to have passed certain thresholds of spiritual development and commitment at different points in the seminary program (in contrast to the open-ended nature of non-seminary spiritual direction)...[109]

1c) Terminate spiritual direction

The *PPF* says, "The spiritual director should notify the rector if the director decides to discontinue spiritual direction with any student or if the student discontinues direction with him."[110] This implies that there might be occasions when a spiritual

---

[108] *Instruction concerning the Criteria for the Discernment of Vocations with regard to Persons with Homosexual Tendencies in view of their Admission to the Seminary and to Holy Orders*, Aug. 31, 2005, no. 3.

[109] no. 132.

[110] no. 135.

director would decide to stop being a seminarian's spiritual director. Such occasions might be:

1. If the seminarian will not take the spiritual director's recommendation to take an important matter to his formator or to a psychologist, for example, the seminarian's viewing of Internet pornography;
2. If the seminarian is not open or honest with the spiritual director;[111] or
3. If the seminarian is obviously unsuitable for priesthood.[112]

If the spiritual director is also the confessor of the seminarian,[113] then it seems that the only reason for which he could terminate spiritual direction would

---

[111] *PPF* no. 132 states, "...a lack of readiness for spiritual direction itself ought to prompt a student to question his continuance in the seminary at this time and seriously to consider withdrawing from the program until he is ready."

[112] See 1b and 1d in this section.

[113] Since the *Ratio*, no. 107, says that it could be fitting, for integral formation, that the spiritual director also be the confessor; and since the *PPF*, no. 120, says that, ideally, the confessor is also the spiritual director, the seminarian will probably choose to have the spiritual director be his confessor also.

The Code of Canon Law does not make such a recommendation. It emphasizes the seminarian's choice of confessor, and adds that the opinion of the seminarian's spiritual director and confessors can never be sought (see c. 240).

be the seminarian's not being open with him.[114]

1d) Reveal a confidence, if an exception to the confidentiality of spiritual direction applies

If an exception to the confidentiality of spiritual direction applies, the spiritual director, unless he is also the confessor of the seminarian, may reveal the confidence.[115] The *PPF* states exceptions to the confidentiality of spiritual direction:

> ...the spiritual director is held to the strictest confidentiality concerning information received in spiritual direction. He may neither reveal it

---

[114] Otherwise, the spiritual director might violate the seal of Confession.

If the spiritual director was not also the confessor, then it seems that he could terminate the spiritual direction for the other reasons suggested above, besides the seminarian's lack of openness, and would not be violating confidentiality (by the termination's being an implicit warning to the rector), because: 1) the *PPF* allows a spiritual director to discontinue spiritual direction; 2) in those other cases besides lack of openness, the seminarian was not truly confiding in him but was being duplicitous; and 3) in those other cases, the moral theology exception to secrecy for matters that "conduce to the spiritual or corporal corruption of the community, or to some grave personal injury" (Summa II-II, Q. 70, A. 1) would apply.

[115] The reasons presented in n.53 would similarly apply to revealing a confidence.

nor use it. The only possible exception to this standard of confidentiality would be the case of grave, immediate, or mortal danger involving the directee or another person. If what is revealed in spiritual direction coincides with the celebration of the Sacrament of Penance... then the absolute strictures of the seal of confession hold, and no information may be revealed or used.[116]

The Congregation for Catholic Education's report on the visitation of U.S. seminaries[117] criticized seminaries for listing exceptions to the confidentiality of spiritual direction, saying "Other seminaries dilute the confidential nature of the internal forum: the spiritual directors and students are presented with a list of 'exceptions' to the confidentiality of spiritual direction (even if it is always emphasized that the seal of confession is inviolable)." Since the Congregation approved the *PPF*, it seems that the visitation report should have clarified whether it had considered in its criticism the exceptions in the *PPF*.[118]

If a seminarian indicated to his spiritual director that he was sexually attracted to children, by saying, for example, that he was accessing child

---

[116] no. 134.

[117] p. 14.

[118] The Congregation for Clergy approved the PPF in 2015, so the exceptions are still approved by the Apostolic See.

pornography on the Internet; or that he had sexually abused a child, the *PPF* would not require the spiritual director to maintain the confidentiality, since the seminarian would pose a danger to children. *PPF* says, "Any credible evidence in the candidate of a sexual attraction to children necessitates an immediate dismissal from the seminary."[119]

2) Annual evaluations by peers

The rector is to obtain annual peer evaluations on each seminarian: "The opinion of the candidate's class companions, given in an absolutely secret and personal form, in which a positive or negative opinion concerning the suitability of the candidate is expressed clearly, together with reasons for that opinion."[120]

---

[119] no. 96.

[120] Congregation for Divine Worship and the Discipline of the Sacraments, Scrutinies, Enclosure II ("Documentation for the Scrutiny for each (Liturgical) Stage in the Candidate's Progress toward the Priesthood"), no. 7.

The "Scrutinies" are presented in a Circular Letter, with five "Enclosures," by the Congregation for Divine Worship and the Discipline of the Sacraments, "Scrutinies regarding the Suitability of Candidates for Orders," (Nov. 10, 1997) (Prot. n. 589/97). The Enclosures list the documentation, procedures, and guidelines for the preparation of reports necessary in order to ordain candidates to the priesthood.

The *PPF* gives a description of the process of obtaining peer evaluations:

> Peer evaluations are recommended as helpful in the evaluation process. Such evaluations should be conducted in a responsible and confidential manner. Seminarians completing peer evaluations should be exhorted to do so with honesty and in a spirit of charity. Positive or negative opinions concerning the suitability of a peer for advancement should be expressed clearly. [121]

3) The seminarian's openness, in an atmosphere of trust

The seminarian needs to be open and docile with his formators in order to be formed to be suitable to be a priest.

The *Ratio* indicates that the seminarian should be open and trusting with his formators:

1. "In the process of formation, it is necessary that the seminarian should know himself and let himself be known, relating to the formators with sincerity and transparency. Personal accompaniment, which has *docibilitas* to the Holy Spirit as its goal, is an indispensable means of formation."[122]

2. "In order for this training to be fruitful, it is

---

[121] no. 277.
[122] no. 45.

important that every seminarian be aware of his own life history, and be ready to share it with his formators...."[123]

3. "The seminarian is required to be docile, to review his own life constantly and to be open to fraternal correction, so as to respond ever more fully to the workings of grace."[124]

4. "Conversations with formators should be regular and frequent. In this way the seminarian will be able gradually to conform himself to Christ, docile to the action of the Spirit...."[125]

It is similarly indicated in documents by the Congregation for Catholic Education:

1. "The success of the formational relationship depends in great part on these three capacities. On the one hand, there is the educator with his role of counseling and guiding, and on the other there is the student called to adopt an attitude of free initiative."[126]

---

[123] no. 94.

[124] no. 58.

[125] no. 46.

[126] "Directives concerning the Preparation of Seminary Educators" in *Origins*, Jan. 27,1994, vol. 23, no. 32; #37; also published as "Directives on the Preparation of Formators in Seminaries," in *Enchiridion Vaticanum* 13 (1996) 3224-3253. The third "capacity"

2. "The candidate is asked to be sincerely and trustingly open with his formators. Only by sincerely allowing them to know him can he be helped on that spiritual journey that he himself is seeking by entering the seminary....Important, and often determinant in overcoming possible misunderstandings, will be both the educational atmosphere between students and formators – marked by openness and transparency..."[127]

3. The candidate:

    ...must offer himself trustingly to the discernment of the Church, of the Bishop who calls him to orders, to the rector of the seminary, of his spiritual director and of the other seminary educators to whom the Bishop or major superior has entrusted the task of forming future priests....the spirit of truth, loyalty, and openness that must characterize the personality of him who believes he is called to serve Christ and his Church in the ministerial priesthood.[128]

For religious seminarians, the Code of Canon Law

---

seems to be pedagogical sense on the part of the educator (formator).

[127] *Guidelines for the Use of Psychology...*, no. 12.

[128] *Instruction concerning the Criteria for the Discernment of Vocations with regard to Persons with Homosexual Tendencies...*, Aug. 31, 2005, no. 3.

says (c. 630 §5), "Members are to approach superiors with trust, to whom they can freely and on their own initiative open their minds."

The formators should "guarantee an atmosphere of trust, so that the candidate can open up and participate with conviction in the work of discernment and accompaniment, offering 'his own convinced and heartfelt co-operation'."[129] The *Ratio* says in this regard:

> A necessary element in the process of accompaniment is mutual trust. The programme of formation should explore and outline the concrete ways in which this trust can be encouraged and safeguarded. Above all, those conditions should be sought and fostered, which can, in some way, create a peaceful climate of trust and mutual confidence: fraternity, empathy, understanding, the ability to listen and to share, and especially a coherent witness of life.[130]

The *Ratio* also says, "Certain formative instruments should be adopted for community formation and for a better knowledge of the individual seminarians, such as: sincere and open communication, exchange, review of life, fraternal correction, and community programmes."[131]

---

[129] *Guidelines for the Use of Psychology...*, no. 2 (quoting *Pastores dabo vobis*, n. 69b).

[130] no. 47.

[131] no. 90.

The *PPF* also expects seminarians to be open with their formators and rector, as it says, "Seminaries should expect of seminarians a spirit of joyful trust, open dialogue, and generous cooperation with those in authority...."[132] An example of this in the *PPF* is the annual self-evaluation done by the seminarian with his formator:

> A seminarian's self-evaluation can be a valuable instrument. Seminarians should prepare such evaluations with an honest and candid examination of themselves in the areas of human, spiritual, intellectual, and pastoral formation. They should recognize their strengths and weaknesses, and positive qualities as well as areas of needed growth. It is the responsibility of the seminarian to show positive qualities that recommend his advancement in formation. This self-evaluation is done best in consultation with a formation advisor/mentor.[133]

A seminarian could talk with his formator about intimate matters, even if he had told them to his spiritual director, because:

1. The seminarian is not under an obligation of secrecy about the matters (his spiritual

---

[132] no. 101.
[133] no. 276.

director is under the obligation of secrecy).

2. Seminarians are to be open and transparent with their formators and the rector.[134]

3. Church documents on priestly formation explicitly permit this:

   a) The *Ratio* states, "... in a relationship of sincere dialogue and mutual trust, the seminarian is obliged to reveal to his formators — to the Bishop, the Rector, the Spiritual Director and to other formators — doubts or difficulties he should have in this regard [homosexual tendencies]"[135]

   b) In *Guidelines for the Use of Psychology*, the Congregation for Catholic Education states:

   c) "Should the spiritual director request that the candidate undergo a psycho-logical consultation, it is desirable that the candidate, as well as informing the spiritual director himself about the results of the consultation, will likewise inform the external-forum formator, especially if the spiritual director himself will have invited him to do this."[136] (Both the spiritual director and the formator would have the same

---

[134] See above, and section C4d below.

[135] no. 200.

[136] no. 14.

confidential information revealed by the seminarian.)

d) The *PPF* says, "Care should be taken that issues of human formation that properly belong to the external forum are not limited to the spiritual direction relationship for their resolution."[137] This indicates that the seminarian should talk with his formator or the rector about the same matter as he had talked about with his spiritual director.

4. There is an overlapping of roles of the formator and the spiritual director.[138]

4) Actions of the formator

The formator is to get to know the seminarian in various ways.

4a) Observe and ask about behavior

The formator's role of observing and asking questions about behavior, on a superficial level, could be described as monitoring. "Formation mentors/ advisors monitor seminarians assigned to them in all four areas of formation and they assist in the

---

[137] no. 131.
[138] See section C4d2C below.

evaluation process."[139];

> [Regarding the annual written evaluations of a seminarian done by formators] "There should be accountability in the external forum for seminarians' participation in spiritual exercises of the seminary and their growth as men of faith. Within the parameters of the external forum, habits of prayer and personal piety are also areas of accountability.... — Fidelity to regular spiritual direction[140] and regular celebration of the Sacrament of Penance and a habit of spiritual reading..."[141]

Along with the monitoring role, the formator may ask the seminarian about his behavior or manifest troubles, such as the seminarian's looking troubled, or his being late for a scheduled activity, or a report that he was seen using the Internet late at night.

The formator's role of observing and asking questions about behavior is more than on a superficial level. The formator should systematically observe the behavior and habits of the seminarian, and offer him in-depth feedback on

---

[139] *PPF*, no. 328.

[140] Seminaries require the seminarian to see his spiritual director on a regular basis (at least monthly). See *Ratio* no. 107; Congregation for Clergy, "The Priest, Minister of Divine Mercy: An Aid for Confessors and Spiritual Directors" (Libreria Editrice Vaticana, 2011) 68; *PPF*, nos. 110, 127.

[141] *PPF*, no. 280.

them. The feedback is to be about seminarians' "general demeanor, their relational capacities and styles, their maturity, their capacity to assume the role of a public person and leader in a community, and their appropriation of the human virtues that make them 'men of communion.'"[142] The formator is to "single out which of his [the seminarian's] attitudes and inclinations are to be encouraged, which are to be corrected and the most significant traits of his personality."[143] The formator is to "offer encouragement, support, and challenge along the formational path."[144] This might include "personal mentoring or, at times, coaching."[145]

For this in-depth role, the formator needs skill in perceiving and evaluating:

> ...the sensitivity and psychological prepara-
> tion that will allow him, insofar as possible, to
> perceive the candidate's true motivations, to
> discern the barriers that stop him integrating
> human and Christian maturity, and to pick up
> on any psychopathic disturbances present in the
> candidate. The formator must accurately and
> very prudently evaluate the candidate's history.
> ...must see the candidate's strong and weak

---

[142] *PPF*, no. 80.

[143] The Congregation for Catholic Education, *Directives concerning the Preparation of Seminary Educators [Formators], Origins*, Jan. 27, 1994, vol. 23, no. 32, #57.

[144] *PPF*, no. 80

[145] *PPF*, no. 80

points, as well as the level of awareness that the candidate has of his own problems. Lastly, the formator must discern the candidate's capacity for controlling his own behavior in responsibility and freedom.[146]

4b) Use the psychologist's report

The information from a psychological evaluation or report on the seminarian is to be made available to formators,[147] and formators can and should use the

---

[146] *Guidelines for the Use of Psychology*..., no. 4.

The *PPF* (no. 92) states, "Formators should be attentive in discerning whether there is a merely formal and external respect given to the formation demands placed upon those entrusted to their care. Such an attitude would not help their integral growth but rather would make them accustomed, more or less unconsciously, to a purely servile and self-serving obedience."

[147] "In a spirit of reciprocal trust and in co-operation with his own formation, the candidate can be invited freely to give his written consent so that the expert in the psychological sciences... can communicate the results of the consultation to the formators indicated by the candidate himself." Congregation for Catholic Education, *Guidelines*..., no. 13.

The *Ratio* (no. 195) says, "...those authorised to have knowledge of the information provided by the expert are: the Bishop (of the Diocese of the candidate, and the Bishop responsible for the Seminary, if different), the Rector (of the Seminary in which formation occurs, and also of the diocesan Seminary, if different), and the Spiritual Director." One presumes, based on *Ratio* nos.

psychological report in doing formation and in vocational discernment.[148] The formators should use the information "to sketch out a general picture of the candidate's personality, and to infer the appropriate indications for the candidate's further path of formation or for his admission to ordination"[149]; and to learn ways to support the development of human, especially relational, qualities needed in the seminarian.[150]

---

192 and 193 (quoted above), that the *Ratio* would agree that the rector, with the previous consent of the candidate, would share the psychologist's report with the formators.

The *PPF* states that the applicant should understand that the testing results will be shared with select seminary personnel in a way that permits a thorough review. *PPF*, no. 52.

[148] "...it is appropriate to obtain a psychological evaluation, both at the time of admission to the Seminary, and subsequently, when it seems useful to the formators." (*Ratio*, no. 193); "The contribution of the psychological sciences has generally been shown to be a considerable help to formators, as they are responsible for vocational discernment. This scientific contribution allows the character and personality of the candidates to be known better and it enables formation to be adapted more fittingly to the needs of the individual: *"It is useful for the Rector and other formators to be able to count on the co-operation of experts in the psychological sciences....* [quoting *Guidelines in the Use of Psychology..., no. 6*]" (*Ratio*, no. 192)

[149] *Guidelines..., no.13.*

[150] See *Guidelines..., no. 5.*

The *PPF*, in the context of psychological records, says that the rector is to maintain "the traditional distinction between the internal and external forum."[151] There seems, however, to be no official "traditional distinction." The other Church documents on priestly formation do not use the

---

The formator is to use the information to help the candidate achieve the growth necessary to become a 'man of communion.'" *PPF*, no. 57.

[151] *PPF* no. 57. "Concerning the results of psychological testing and other confidential materials, the seminary must observe all legal requirements, inform the applicant in writing of his specific rights to privacy and confidentiality, and utilize appropriate release forms. Throughout the admission process and, if accepted, after entrance into the seminary, the candidate's right to privacy should be respected and the careful management of confidential materials is to be observed. This is especially true in the case of sharing confidential information with a team of formators, while at the same time ensuring that those charged with the candidate's growth and integration have the clear and specific information they need so that they can help the candidate achieve the growth necessary to become a 'man of communion.' The rector must observe a careful vigilance that protects the privacy and reputation of the seminarian in his relationship with the formation faculty. The traditional distinction between internal and external forum is to be maintained. Clear policies must be enunciated concerning who may have access to any of the admissions materials. Clear directives must be in place to determine any further use of psychological testing results or other admissions materials for formation or even counseling purposes."

term "external forum."[152] The *PPF* does not allude to any other Church document outside of itself in regard to the "traditional distinction."

This *PPF* sentence about maintaining the distinction between forums is also unnecessary, since that same paragraph (no. 57) elaborates on the steps to be taken to protect the candidate's right to privacy. The sentence also seems inconsistent, since:

1. The psychologist is not in the internal forum. The Church documents on priestly formation do not include the psychologist in the internal forum. As the Congregation for Education explicitly stated in its visitation report, "There is confusion, in places, as to what the internal forum is (it covers only sacramental confession and spiritual direction; psychological counseling may be confidential, but it is not internal forum)."[153]

2. The psychologist's report is not in the internal forum. The *PPF* allows the psychologist's report to be released (with the candidate's consent) to formators.

---

[152] See section C4d2C, n.139, below, regarding the one exception.

[153] no. 6, p.14.

4c) Use the peer evaluations

It seems that seminary rectors, in practice, give to formators a copy of the evaluations of the seminarian by his peers, at least in summary form, for the purposes of formation and vocational discernment.

4d) Frequent and regular conversations with the seminarian

4d1) Help him to train his character and come to self-knowledge

The *Ratio* says that the formator is to have frequent and regular conversations with the seminarian, to help him become aware of his condition, talents, and frailties; to educate him in the truth of his being and to foster a sincere gift of self:

> Conversations with formators should be regular and frequent. In this way the seminarian will be able gradually to conform himself to Christ, docile to the action of the Spirit. Such accompaniment must bring together all the aspects of the human person, training him in listening, in dialogue, in the true meaning of obedience and in interior freedom. It is the task of every formator, each according to his proper responsibilities, to assist the seminarian in becoming aware of his condition, of the talents that he has received, and of his frailties, so that

he can become ever more receptive to the action of grace.[154]

....This process of [human] formation is intended to educate the person in the truth of his being, in freedom and in self-control. It is meant to overcome all kinds of individualism, and to foster the sincere gift of self, opening him to generous dedication to others.[155]

The *Ratio* says that the seminarian is to share his life with his formators:

In order for this training to be fruitful, it is important that every seminarian be aware of his own life history, and be ready to share it with his formators. This would include especially his experience of childhood and adolescence, the influence that his family and his relatives have exercised upon him, his ability to establish mature and well balanced interpersonal relationships, or his lack thereof, and his ability to handle positively moments of solitude. Such information will be helpful for choosing the most fitting pedagogical means, both for an assessment of the journey thus far and for a better understanding of any moments of regression or of difficulty.[156]

---

[154] no. 46.

[155] no. 63.

[156] no. 94.

The Congregation for Catholic Education, in its *Directives concerning the Preparation of Seminary Educators*, states that the formator is to have frequent contacts and a real and profound communication with the seminarian, to help the seminarian to know himself in depth, and to measure his progress and orient his goals:

> The success of the formational relationship depends in great part on these three capacities. On the one hand, there is the educator with his role of counseling and guiding, and on the other there is the student called to adopt an attitude of free initiative. In this relationship a great deal depends on psychologically well-chosen and well-spaced-out interventions of the educator. It is necessary to avoid behavior which is too passive and fails to promote dialogue, but also to avoid an excessive invasiveness which may block it. The capacity for real and profound communication succeeds in touching the center of the person of the student; it is not satisfied with an external perception, in essence dangerously deceptive, of the values which are communicated; it stirs up vital dynamisms of capacity for relationships that bring into play the most authentic and radical motivations of the person, who feels accepted, stimulated and appreciated. Such contacts should be frequent, to measure progress, to orient goals, adapting the formational assistance to the pace of each one and succeeding in this way in individualizing the level at which the true

problems and difficulties of each person are grasped. [157]

...The educator should be sufficiently prepared as not to be deceived or to deceive regarding a presumed consistency and maturity of the student. ...An attentive and refined examination from a good knowledge of the human sciences is necessary in order to go beyond appearances and the superficial level of motivations and behavior, and to help the seminarian to know himself in depth, to accept himself with serenity and to correct himself and to mature, starting from real, not illusory, roots and from the "heart" of his person. [158]

This implies that the formator is to talk to the seminarian about his personal problems.

The Congregation for Catholic Education, in its *Guidelines for the Use of Psychology*, also indicates that the formator is to help the seminarian to train his character and foster the sincere gift of self:

Formators need to be adequately prepared to carry out a discernment that... must allow for the candidate to be accompanied on his path to acquiring those moral and theological virtues, which are necessary for living, in coherence and interior freedom, the total gift of his life, so as to

---

[157] no. 37.
[158] no. 57.

be a "servant of the Church as communion." [159]

The CIVCSVA, in its *Directives on Formation in Religious Institutes* [for religious], states, "They [teachers] should also accompany religious along the paths of the Lord by means of direct and regular dialogue, always respecting the proper role of the confessor and spiritual director in the strict sense of the words."[160]

In regard to evaluations of a seminarian by his formator and others, the *PPF* states:

> each seminary should ensure ...that the seminarians are apprised of their progress as early as possible in their formation, particularly if there are concerns; that the formation advisor/mentor regularly communicates with the seminarian; ...The process of evaluation should be conducted in an atmosphere of mutual trust and confidence. It should promote the continued growth of the seminarian in the four dimensions of formation.[161]

The formator talks with the seminarian periodically (in the United States, at least monthly) about evaluations of the seminarian, including his self-evaluation. The *PPF* says that the seminarian's self-

---

[159] no. 3 (quoting *Pastores dabo vobis*, n.16e).
[160] no. 30.
[161] no. 274.

evaluation "is done best in consultation with a formation advisor/mentor."[162]

Based on the above quotes, the formator should not fear when a seminarian wants to open his heart to him (although not in Confession, so that the formator is not bound by the seal of Confession), and should not discourage a seminarian from doing so; should not tell him that such matter belongs only in spiritual direction.

While it seems that the formator can discuss with the seminarian any matter that the seminarian brings up, or any matter about which the formator learns from other than from the seminarian, it seems that the formator cannot ask the seminarian about matters of sin to learn (discover) his sins. The Congregation for Catholic Education, in its visitation report, criticized formation advisers for asking about matters of sin, saying: "There have also been cases of formation advisors invading the internal forum, asking about matters of sin"[163]; and "The internal forum needs to be better safeguarded.... In places, seminarians are being asked to reveal (in formation advising, in psychological counseling, in public confessions of faults, etc.) matters of sin, which belong instead to the internal forum."[164]

It seems that this prohibition against asking about matters of sin must be narrowly construed

---

[162] no. 276.

[163] p. 12, no. 5.

[164] p. 14, no. 6

to mean that the formator cannot ask the seminarian to divulge his sins or whether he has done particular (named) sins. The reasons for this narrow interpretation are:

1. Part of the role of the formator is to help the seminarian to become aware of his frailties, to know himself in depth. As quoted above, "It is the task of every formator, each according to his proper responsibilities, to assist the seminarian in becoming aware of his condition, of the talents that he has received, and of his frailties, so that he can become ever more receptive to the action of grace."[165] "[The educator should] help the seminarian to know himself in depth, to accept himself with serenity and to correct himself and to mature, starting from real, not illusory, roots and from the 'heart' of his person."[166]   He [the formator] must see the candidate's strong and weak points, as well as the level of awareness that the candidate has of his own problems.[167]

2. The *Ratio* recommends fraternal correction and other community formation programs: "Certain formative instruments should be adopted for community formation and for a

---

[165] *Ratio*, no. 46.

[166] *Directives concerning the preparation of seminary educators* ("*Directives*"), no. 57

[167] *Guidelines for the Use of Psychology*, no. 4.

better knowledge of the individual semi-narians, such as: sincere and open communication, exchange, review of life, fraternal correction, and community programmes."[168]

3. Some sins are obvious and could not be considered as private matters. If a seminarian punched another seminarian, it probably would be a matter of sin, but it would not be confidential, since it would be evident to the victim and to anyone else who saw it. The formator could ask the seminarian about it.

4. The spiritual director might refer the seminarian to the formator for a resolution of a matter which is a matter of sin, such as viewing pornography.[169]

5. The rector and formators need to deal quickly with issues that make a seminarian unsuitable to be a priest.[170] For example, the *Ratio* states, "... in a relationship of sincere dialogue and mutual trust, the seminarian is obliged to reveal to his formators — to the Bishop, the Rector, the Spiritual Director and to other formators — doubts or difficulties he should have in this regard [homosexual tendencies]."[171] If a seminarian had some homosexual experiences in the past, the formator could ask him if there

---

[168] no. 90.

[169] See section C1a above.

[170] See section B3 above.

[171] no. 200.

were any further episodes to ascertain whether he is suitable for the priesthood. The Congregation for Education, in its visitation report stated, "...here and there some case or other of immorality —again, usually homosexual behavior — continues to show up. However, in the main, the superiors now deal with these issues promptly and appropriately."[172]

It seems that formators and the rector can and should ask the seminarian about matters of sin that have been indicated to them.

4d2) Does not conflict with the role of the spiritual director

This role of the formator (in the previous subsection) does not conflict with the role of the spiritual director because:

1. There are important differences in their roles;
2. The confidential matters themselves are not in the internal forum; and
3. The Church documents on priestly formation indicate there is an overlap in their roles.

---

[172] p. 11.

4d2A) Differences in the roles

There are importance differences between the role of the formator and the role of the spiritual director:

1. The formator is not to hear seminarians' confessions.[173]
2. The spiritual director may not reveal confidences or give his opinion about the seminarian.[174]
3. The spiritual director directs the seminarian's relationship with God and discernment of God's will, and he helps the seminarian to live in union with Christ. The Church documents on priestly formation indicate this role of the spiritual director:

The *Ratio*:

"Spiritual formation is directed at nourishing and sustaining communion with God and with our brothers and sisters, in the friendship of Jesus the Good Shepherd, and with an attitude of docility to the Holy Spirit."[175]

"The heart of spiritual formation is personal

---

[173] See *PPF*, no. 120.

[174] See sections A2 and C1 above.

[175] no. 101.

union with Christ, which is born of, and nourished in, a particular way by prolonged and silent prayer."[176]

"The Spiritual Director...helps the seminarian to welcome the divine calling and to develop a free and generous response."[177]

The Congregation for Catholic Education, in its *Directives*:

"The role of the spiritual director or father is also very demanding. The responsibility for the spiritual journey of the seminarians in the internal forum falls upon him."[178]; and "The spiritual director, with his duty of offering to the community and to individuals, in the confidential relationship of spiritual direction, a sure guidance in the search for the will of God and in vocational discernment...The preparation of the spiritual director for his multiple duties and above all for that of care for the formation of the consciences of the students...the person who receives [spiritual] direction should live it as a means and stimulus for his own journey of faith and obedience to the will of God."[179]

---

[176] no. 102.

[177] no. 136.

[178] no. 44 (The *Ratio*, no. 136, quotes this last sentence.)

[179] no. 61.

The *PPF*: "Each seminarian is encouraged to have a regular confessor, who ideally is also his spiritual director..."[180]

In regard to members of religious institutes:

Code c. 630,§1: "Superiors are to recognize the due freedom of their members regarding the sacrament of penance and direction of conscience..."; and CIVCSVA's *Directives on Formation in Religious Institutes* indicates the main responsibilities of the spiritual director are: "discernment of God's action; the accompaniment of the religious in the ways of God, the nourishing of life with solid doctrine and the practice of prayer..."[181]

4d2B) Confidential matters themselves not in the internal forum

The formator, in discussing personal matters of the seminarian with him, is not conflicting with the role of the spiritual director. The confidential matters themselves are not in the internal forum. It is the spiritual director who is in the internal forum.

The *PPF*, in two places (nos. 80 and 328, with the same language in both), says that formators

---

[180] no. 120.
[181] no. 63.

"function exclusively in the external forum and are not to engage in matters that are reserved for the internal forum and the spiritual director." This leads to the question, "What is 'reserved for the internal forum and the spiritual director,' and by whom is it reserved?"

In regard to "the internal forum," Church documents on priestly formation since the Second Vatican Council say that the confessor and spiritual director are in the internal forum, and have not included anyone else.

Disclosures to the spiritual director are in the internal forum, i.e. the spiritual director may not reveal them. The *PPF* states, "...the spiritual director is held to the strictest confidentiality concerning information received in spiritual direction."[182]

Who determines what is "reserved for the internal forum"? It seems that it is the seminarian who determines this. The seminarian decides what is in the internal forum by what he chooses to confide to the spiritual director (and by what he confesses in Confession) and does not tell to others.

The seminarian's self-revelation to the spiritual director binds the spiritual director; no one else. It does not prevent the formator from asking about confidential issues. Since the matters confided to the spiritual director are secret, the formator would not know what they are. The formator could ask the seminarian about anything (other than to ask his

---

[182] no. 134.

sins),[183] and it would be for the seminarian to decide whether or not to answer. The seminarian might choose not to answer because he wanted to speak about it only in spiritual direction. The seminarian might choose to answer, even if he had already spoken to the spiritual director about it, since it is the seminarian himself who determines what is "reserved for the spiritual director." (The seminarian is not bound to confidentiality.)

Some might argue that this interpretation of the statement in *PPF* 80 (and 328) (that formators "are not to engage in matters reserved for the spiritual director") renders the statement meaningless. It does not render the statement meaningless. The interpretation results in the same conclusion as one would reach in applying c. 220. The formator may ask about sensitive issues, but the seminarian can choose not to respond. If he chooses not to respond, then he has, in effect, reserved the matter to the spiritual director. In that case, the formator may not insist (persist), since the matter is reserved (by the seminarian). Canon 220 would lead to the same conclusion (the questioner may not insist on an answer).

This interpretation is supported by the fact that all confidential communications of a seminarian are not "reserved for the internal forum and the spiritual director," as indicated by the following:

(1) The spiritual director might advise a

---

[183] See section C4d1 above.

seminarian to reveal confidential matters to a psychologist or to a formator or the rector.[184]

(2) The self-evaluation that seminarians are to do with their formator could be considered to be confidential information.[185]

(3) Peer evaluations are to be done by the seminarians with honesty, and are confidential information.[186] In seminary practice, the formators receive a copy of them, at least in summary form.

(4) Confidential matters revealed by the seminarian to a psychologist are not in the internal forum.

If the seminarian or candidate to the seminary agrees to a release of psychological information to formators so that the formators can use it in formation, then the formators also have the confidential information.[187]

Consequently, it seems that there are no particular areas (types of matters) that are in themselves "reserved for the internal forum and the spiritual director."

4d2C) Overlap in roles

The Church documents on priestly formation in-

---

[184] See section C1a above.

[185] See section C3 above.

[186] See section C2 above.

[187] See section C4b above.

dicate there is an overlap in the roles of the formator and the spiritual director.

(1) Per the Congregation for Clergy in the *Ratio*

The Congregation for Clergy, in the *Ratio*, allows an overlapping of roles between the formators and the spiritual directors, as indicated by:

a) The Ratio does not repeat or cite the paragraph found in the Congregation for Catholic Education's *Directives* about the need for the spiritual director to guard his duties. The *Directives* say, "The spiritual director is therefore the first guardian of his own identity and of his own duties, which cannot be renounced or substituted for and which can neither be confused with those of the other educators nor improperly substituted for with other types of formational service."[188]

The *Ratio* cites the *Directives* fourteen times, including quoting from the document about the role of the spiritual director, but the *Ratio* does not cite this paragraph, and it would seem that the Congregation for Clergy would disagree with it, based on points (b)-(e) below:

---

[188] no. 61.

b) The *Ratio* describes "formators" as including at least the rector (who is a person not in the internal forum) and the spiritual director, the two minimum formators required by the Code for a seminary.[189] The *Ratio*, in ten passages, speaks of "the spiritual director,"[190] and sometimes lists "formators" separately from "spiritual directors",[191] applying the text to both groups equally. For example, the seminarian must reveal to "his formators—to the Bishop, the Rector, the Spiritual Director and to other formators—" any doubts or difficulties he has in regard to homosexual tendencies.[192]

The *Ratio* indicates that the seminarian is to be open with his formators,[193] and the formator is to have frequent in-depth conversations with the seminarian.[194] The *Ratio*, without distinguishing as to type of formator, says that the seminarian should be transparent with his formators and should converse frequently with them.[195] Every seminarian should be ready to share

---

[189] no. 133.

[190] nos. 63, 65, 84, 88, 96, 107, 133, 134, 136, 200.

[191] nos. 63, 96, 134, 200.

[192] no. 200.

[193] See section C3 above.

[194] See section C4d above.

[195] nos. 45, 46.

his life history with his formators.[196]

c) Every formator is to help the seminarian to become aware of his talents and frailties; to accompany the seminarian to help his human and spiritual growth.[197] Formation is to educate the person in the truth of his being.[198] The *Ratio* talks about conscience formation under human formation: Talking about human formation, the *Ratio* says, "In the moral sphere, it is connected to the requirement that the individual arrive gradually at a well formed conscience."[199]

d) An overlapping of roles is natural if formation is to be integral and not compartmentalized.

The *Ratio* states that the concept of integral formation is of the greatest importance:

> The concept of integral formation is of the greatest importance, since it is the whole person, with all that he is and all that he possesses, who will be at the Lord's service in the Christian community. The one called is an 'integral subject', namely someone who has been previously chosen to attain a

[196] no. 94.
[197] *Ratio*, nos. 46, 49, 63.
[198] *Ratio*, no. 63.
[199] *Ratio*, no. 94.

sound interior life, without divisions or contradictions. It is necessary to adopt an integrated pedagogical model in order to reach this objective...[200]

The *Ratio* indicates that one reason for the importance of integral formation is that grace builds upon nature:

A correct and harmonious spirituality demands a well-structured humanity; indeed, as St. Thomas Aquinas reminds us, *"grace builds upon nature"* it does not supplant nature, but perfects it. Therefore, it is necessary to cultivate humility, courage, common sense, magnanimity, right judgement and discretion, tolerance and transparency, love of truth and honesty.[201]

Human formation, being the foundation of all priestly formation, promotes the integral growth of the person and allows the integration of all its dimensions....psychologically it focuses on the constitution of a stable personality, characterised by emotional balance, self-control and a well-integrated sexuality. In the moral sphere, it is connected to the requirement that the individual arrive gradually at a well formed conscience. This means that he will become a responsible person able to make the

---

[200] no. 92.
[201] no. 93.

right decisions, gifted with right judgement and able to have an objective perception of persons and events....aware of his own talents and learning how to place them at the service of the People of God. ...aware of the social environment, and be helped to improve his capacity for social interaction, so that he can contribute to building up the community in which he lives....[202]

The use of the term "external forum," opposing it to the persons in the internal forum, seems to be contrary to communion in the seminary. It does not seem to promote an integral formation. The *Ratio* mentions the term "internal forum" only once, in no. 136 (see A2 above), and it does not mention "external forum" at all. The Congregation for Catholic Education's documents on priestly formation do not use the term "external forum."[203]

(e) The Congregation for Clergy does not want tension between the seminary spiritual directors

---

[202] no. 94.

[203] It seems that, of all the Church document on priestly formation since the Second Vatican Council, only one, besides the *PPF*, uses the term "external forum," the post-synodal apostolic exhortation *Pastores dabo vobis* by St. Pope John Paul II (1992). *Pastores dabo vobis*, no. 66, similar to *PPF* no. 57 (see section 4b above), says that the priestly community of teachers are to safeguard "the distinctions between internal and external forum," without explaining the distinctions.

and the formators regarding their respective roles, since the *Ratio* emphasizes the importance of communion in the seminary:

"The Seminary community is indeed a family, marked by an atmosphere that favours friendship and fraternity...."[204]; the priest is called to be a "man of communion"[205]; "...Community life in the Seminary is the most suitable context for preparing seminarians for true priestly fraternity. It is the environment in which the aforementioned dimensions come together and interact, and where they attain to mutual harmony and integration."[206]; "...he [the Bishop] should maintain frequent personal contact with those in charge of the seminary, placing his trust in them, so as to encourage them in their task and to foster among them a spirit of full harmony, communion and cooperation."[207]

(2) Per the Congregation for Catholic Education

The Congregation for Catholic Education indicates in its visitation report that there is an overlapping of roles between the formator and the spiritual director, as it says, "...the 'formation advisor,' who acts somewhat like a spiritual director but in the external forum. The advisor follows the can-

---

[204] no. 52.

[205] no. 52.

[206] no. 90.

[207] no. 128.

didate, including by means of frequent dialogues, helping him integrate the four dimensions (human, spiritual, intellectual, pastoral) of priestly formation ...."[208]

(3) Per the USCCB in the *PPF*

In the *PPF*, both the spiritual director and the formator have the roles:

5. to assist the seminarian in vocational discernment,
6. to assist the seminarian to prepare for the reception of ministries and orders, and
7. formation for celibacy. [209]

PPF no. 79, which is in the section on "human formation," states, "Seminary formation in sexuality and celibacy must communicate to priesthood candidates and enable them to appropriate:...The requisite skills for living chastely: ascetical practice, prudent self-mastery, and paths of self-knowledge, such as a regular personal inventory and the examination of conscience...The spiritual path that transforms the experience of loneliness into a holy solitude based on a "strong, lively, and personal love for Jesus Christ..." The *PPF* indicates that the rector and formators have the role of educating the seminarians in under-

---

[208] p. 12, no. 5.
[209] See nos. 77-79, 90-92,103,110,132, 133.

standing sexuality and living chastely,[210] and are to use encouragement, support, and challenge[211]; while "Spiritual formation in celibacy cultivates the evangelical motivations for embracing this commitment and way of life..."[212]

4e3) Application of canon 220

As mentioned above,[213] it would not fit with the role of the formator (described above) to require the formator to ask the seminarian for his consent each time the formator wanted to have a dialogue with him or ask him a personal question.[214] Canon 220 still has application, however. Canon 220 would restrict the formator in that:

1. To protect the seminarian's right to privacy, the formator may not oblige or insist upon the seminarian's answering his questions.[215]

It seems that formators might need training to establish a comfortable rapport with the seminarian

---

[210] nos. 77, 79.

[211] no. 80.

[212] no. 110.

[213] (in section A1)

[214] Nonetheless, since the seminarian's expectations might differ from those of the seminary, it seems advisable for the seminary to obtain from each new seminarian a signed agreement in regard to the seminary's policies. See below, the Conclusion.

[215] See section A1.

so that he is open with the formator. Otherwise, the seminarian might resent questions and be closed. The *Ratio* states:

> Each formator should be possessed of human, spiritual, pastoral and professional abilities and resources, so as to provide the right kind of accompaniment that is balanced and respectful of the freedom and the conscience of the other person, and that will help him in his human and spiritual growth. [216]

The more impersonal the questioning, such as if done in writing rather than in person, or if done to a group rather than to an individual, it seems the more likely that the questioning will meet with resistance and the seminarians might refuse to answer.

The Congregation for Catholic Education talks about the need for the formator to avoid excessive invasiveness that would block dialogue with the seminarian:

> It is necessary to avoid behavior which is too passive and fails to promote dialogue, but also to avoid an excessive invasiveness which may block it. The capacity for real and profound communication succeeds in touching the center of the person of the student...it stirs up vital dynamisms of capacity for relationships that bring into play

---

[216] no. 49.

the most authentic and radical motivations of the person, who feels accepted, stimulated and appreciated.[217]

2. To protect the seminarian's reputation, the formator may not divulge the personal information about the seminarian more than necessary (for formation and determining the suitability of the seminarian).

Conclusion

It is suggested that each seminary have a written policy regarding confidentiality at the seminary, and that each new seminarian be asked to sign a statement that he received a copy and agrees to it.[218] It is suggested that the seminary also put this policy in the seminary handbook.

The policy statement should:

1. Say that the seal of Confession applies to anything said in Confession.
2. Say that everything that is said to the spiritual director outside of Confession may

---

[217] "Directives concerning the Preparation of Seminary Educators" in *Origins*, Jan. 27, 1994, vol. 23, no. 32; #37. See n. 65 above.

[218] Informing the seminarian of the seminary policy is, in effect, obtaining his free consent to the requirement (of revealing his interior life). His consent would be free, since no one is requiring him to (continue to) be a candidate for the priesthood.

not to be revealed by him to anyone unless there is "grave, immediate, or mortal danger involving the directee or another person."[219]

3. Describe the role of the spiritual director.[220]

4. Say that everything that is said to other seminary staff, other than to the spiritual director (and confessor), can be used for the purpose of the seminarian's formation and for determining his suitability as a candidate for priesthood.

5. Say that the seminarian is to be open, trusting, and transparent with his formator, and to meet with him regularly.

6. Describe the role of the formator in helping the seminarian to train his character and come to self-knowledge.[221]

This suggested procedure would clarify matters for the seminarians and confirm their understanding and acceptance of the roles and extent of confidentiality at the seminary.

Sister Joseph Marie Ruessmann, R.S.M., J.D., J.C.D., M.B.A., was the Generalate Secretary of the Religious Sisters of Mercy of Alma, Michigan. She was a canonical consultant for her own and for other institutes, and taught canon law classes to other religious institutes.

---

[219] *PPF*, no. 134.

[220] See section C4d2.

[221] See section C4d.

ABOUT THE AUTHOR

 Sister Marysia Weber, R.S.M., D.O., is a Religious Sister of Mercy of Alma, Michigan. She graduated from MSU-COM in 1983 and completed a medical internship at Pontiac Osteopathic Hospital in Michigan in 1984. She completed her residency in psychiatry at the Mayo Clinic in Rochester, Minnesota in 1987 and her fellowship in consultation-liaison psychiatry at the Mayo Clinic in Rochester, Minnesota in 1988. She is certified by the American Board of Psychiatry and Neurology. She completed a Master's degree in Theology from Notre Dame, South Bend, Indiana in 1997. She practiced in her religious institute's multi-disciplinary medical clinic, Sacred Heart Mercy Health Care Center in Alma, MI, from 1988-2014. She became the Director of the Office of

Consecrated Life for the Archdiocese of Saint Louis in 2014. She currently serves as a member of the Saint Louis Archdiocesan Review Board, the Child Safety Committee, is involved with Project Rachel, collaborates with the Office of Laity and Family Life and is a member of the Catholic Medical Association. She also serves as Adjunct Clinical Instructor in the Department of Psychiatry at Washington University School of Medicine in Saint Louis, Missouri.

She offers workshops on a variety of topics including human attachment, boundaries and character development, depression and anxiety, dialogue and conflict resolution, as well as on social media and its effects on the brain for clergy, seminarians, women's and men's religious communities, parents, teachers and students. She is a formator within her own religious community. She presents on Internet pornography addiction—a Catholic approach to treatment to bishops, clergy, seminarians, religious communities, and laity throughout the United States and Europe. She presented to the U.S. Bishops in Dallas TX in 1992 on "Pedophilia and Other Addictions". She was a member of the USCCB Ad Hoc Committee on Sexual Abuse in 1994-1995. Sister Marysia has presented to the Curia, Vatican City State on "Sexual Abuse of Minors by Clergy in North America" in 2002. She has served as a psychological expert consultant for the Secretariat of Clergy, Consecrated Life and Vocations, USCCB. Her publications include: "Medical Aspects of

Addiction"; "The Roman Catholic Church and the Sexual Abuse of Minors by Priests and Religious in the United States and Canada: What Have We Learned? Where Are We Going?"; "Pornography, Electronic Media and Priestly Formation"; Her papers in *Seminary Journal* include: "Significant Markers of Human Maturation Applied to the Selection and Formation of Seminarians"; "The Discernment of a Priestly Vocation and the Expertise of Psychiatry and Psychology"; and "Internet Pornography and Priestly Formation: Medium and Content Collide With the Human Brain".

Made in the USA
Columbia, SC
01 March 2022